I Know My Shoes Are Untied. Mind Your Own Business!

Phil La Duke

An Iconoclast's View of Workers' Safety

ISBN: 978-1-945853-12-8

Printed in the of America.

FIRST EDITION

TESTIMONIALS

"Chris Rock once said: *"You can only offend me if you mean something to me"*. Phil's writing doesn't pull punches and may be a bit like someone swinging a bag of broken glass in a crowded room but if his words cut deep and gouge a lot of nerves it's only because he has the insight and courage to articulate what many of us are thinking and, for the rest, still struggling with weird feelings, he puts his gnarly finger right on it. People love him because he has empathy and vents on their behalf, people hate him because he has figured them out, exposed them, challenged their worldview and sent their cognitive dissonance into meltdown. Either way, Phil's writing means something to everyone. He has inspired and completely changed the trajectory and style of my own writing. In the words of another safety literary legend and fellow Phil Fan, the late George Robotham: *"It would be a boring world if everybody agreed with me"*.

—Dave Collins, Creator, Editor, and Publisher https://safetyrisk.net/

"Phil's passion comes through in virtually everything he writes. He is an outspoken advocate for employee engagement and respect for workers"

—Dr. Paul Marciano, Best selling author of Carrots and Sticks Don't Work: Build a Culture of Employee Engagement with the Principles of Respect and Super Teams:Using the Principles of Respect to Unleash Explosive Business Performance

"Phil La Duke is an original. After Phil they broke the mold. Certainly his thoughts and ideas on workplace safety and health fit no mold. Phil is no safety drone. His writing is provocative, sometime blunt, sometimes insulting, sometimes raw. His is an outsider's take, almost an outlaw's take, on what is good, bad and ugly about current workplace safety thinking and practices. It's a perspective you won't find anywhere else."

—Dave Johnson, Editor. ISHN magazine

"Phil La Duke has devoted his career to industrial safety. He knows the importance of doing an unglamorous job well and what goes terribly wrong when people don't. He is angry about all the right things.

—Peter Page, contributed content editor Entrepreneur magazine

Phil LaDuke truly shatters the decades-old mindsets of safety professionals that have mired the profession in ideological adherence to accident safety practices, while stifling the introduction of innovative approaches. Provocative as Phil is, he brings a refreshing counterbalance to the safety conversation and makes us think. Indeed, Phil is the "Dirty Jobs Mike Rowe" of the safety profession.

—James E. Leemann, Ph.D.

ACKNOWLEDGEMENTS

There are so many people who have helped me through years of support—family, friends, coworkers—seriously too many to mention and too many unstable and potentially dangerous to slight by leaving them out, so instead I would like to point out those who were of absolutely no help at all:

My elementary school teachers
My high school teachers (especially Sister Grace and Father Miller who both said I would never make anything of myself)
The people of Finland
The emergency room personnel at the hospital who almost killed me through negligence
The original cast of the Broadway Musical Rent
My stalkers and detractors
Internet Trolls

The rest of you on both sides know who you are so thanks for everything or thanks for nothing.

INTRODUCTION AND FORWARD

Whenever I buy a book I skip the introduction and forward. Who gives a shit? Well now that I'm forced to write one I can't say I am too motivated. So instead I wrote some new material. It's better than this tripe that I am writing now.... Well since apparently some of you are still reading I might as well use this opportunity to say this: if you agree with everything I say than you are a mindless as a lemur addicted to Percocet. I make some good points, sure, but the last thing the world needs is another safety drone, unable to think for itself. For those of you who are open-minded there's some great stuff in here. For those of you looking to take offense look no further. For those of you looking for steamy sex scenes, put this book down and step away from the bookshelf. For those of you looking for something to color, there's a drawing of a hummingbird I drew. For those of you looking to expand your consciousness...hell I don't even know where you can get quality LSD anymore, but you could always shred this book and smoke it I suppose, I would try this at least 15 times. So, whatever you're looking for I hope you find it here, but if not, I'm not really going to lose any sleep over it. Anyway, thanks for buying the book (NOTE: If you borrowed this book buy your own copy you cheap bastard.) Enjoy the book; it was a pain in the ass to write.

Phil La Duke

I Know My Shoes Are Untied: Mind Your Own Business

When I first spoke to my publisher she and I had agreed to compile 20 or 30 of my blog posts into a book. She said since the content was already written, all I needed to do was think of a title and come up with some idea of what the cover should look like. She gave me one instruction: under NO CIRCUMSTANCES was I to allow another soul to edit my work. To be sure it needed editing, while I've spent plenty of time consternating uptight safety fossils with my misspellings and stream of consciousness grammar just for the malicious fun of it, I wanted my book to be taut and well executed. The odd typo, my publisher explained, would be caught by her team as the book was typeset, but she didn't want anyone to tamper with my frenetic pace and a voice just at the razor's edge of sanity. I immediately told her I wanted to call the book, *I Know My Shoes Are Untied, Mind Your Own Damned Business: An Iconoclast's View of Safety* but as she explained the business realities of publishing as it pertained to having the word "Damned" in the title and how it might limit our sales opportunities I agreed to the current title (what with me being more greedy than proud).

I have been accused of a lot of things and most of them justly. One can't go around calling people names, being insulting, and behaving boorishly without ruffling the delicate feathers of the more sensitive of readers. Worker safety is important to me. I have written about the loss of my brother-in-law and father to industrial illnesses and the butcher's bill of friends and relatives who sacrificed their lives for their jobs.

I don't believe anyone ever should have to choose between their job or their life, so I believe what we in the safety profession do (although some of us do a poor and misguided job of it) is exceedingly important.

If all this is true, how then, did I come up with such a provocative title?

I hate tying my shoes. Maybe I never learned to tie them correctly, but they never seem to stay tied. I recall an episode of the Sopranos where they are about to eat and Paulie Walnuts heads to the bathroom to wash his hands, Silvio asks where he was going and Paulie tells him to wash his hands. Silvio protests that Paulie just came from the restroom. Paulie explained to the guys that, while yes, he did indeed just come from the restroom he then bent over and tied his shoes. He gave a fairly graphic and gross description of the body fluids that his shoelaces had sloshed through and went and washed his hands.

I hate the feel of my shoelaces and feel compelled to wash my hands after every time I tied them. When I first started working as a consultant in a factory, the safety guy was always on me because my shoes were untied. Finally, he said to me, "La Duke, the next time I see you with untied shoes I'm putting you out of the plant." To this day I don't know if he had the authority to do that, but I took the path of least resistance and went out and bought loafers (despite the fact that the name hit a bit too close to home). Problem solved.

I've thought a lot about that day, and I notice every time someone says, "your shoes are untied" or "watch out you don't trip on your shoelaces" I smile and offer a polite thank you and begrudgingly time my shoes. I have been walking around with untied shoes for over five decades and have never tripped on my untied shoelaces. Furthermore, I don't know anyone who has been injured tripping on their shoelaces. I haven't even heard of a cautionary urban legend where someone walked around with untied shoes and fell. Hell, if the problem was so prevalent why didn't Aesop write a fable about it?

It's nice that people warn me about my untied shoes, and I don't really want them to mind their own business, but it's got me thinking about how easy it is to have someone confront you about something minor and how difficult it is for all parties to have a confrontation about something more serious.

A couple of hours ago a failed science experiment of a man blew through a stop sign and I shouted, "that's a stop sign" instead of flipping me off, this dullard throws his SUV into a full 360° turn runs two more stop signs and glares at me and shouts, "what did you say to me?" I told him that a stop sign meant drivers had to stop. He countered with "I looked and there was no one around so mind your own business" I told him that this is my neighborhood and safety is, IN FACT, my business at which expletives were exchanged and he jumped out of his SUV and started chest bumping me. I could see in his eyes that he wasn't about to do anything, but I calmly reminded him that he had just physically assaulted me and I could have him arrested. He yelled some more, so I calmly took down his plate number (which I later sent to the police). The police in my community don't put up with this kind of crap and assured me they would dispatch him with all due haste and appropriate measures. In my community, the police truly do serve and protect and I have every confidence that when they catch up with him justice will be served. Oh, and here's a tip, if you go around assaulting people, you probably shouldn't have a vanity plate, but then this guy was apparently made up of steroids and chicken shit, so brains weren't his strong suit.

I'm not a hero or even someone who behaves admirably, but as the police officer told me, "if you let the little stuff go it turns into big stuff"; so I confront the little stuff. I poke and I prod and I provoke. I want people to think about their actions and I want them to question their long-standing beliefs. The world is always changing, and it seems that every day there is another threat to safety in the workplace and as Einstein said, "you can't solve problems using the same thinking that created them" and that is as true in safety as it is anywhere else.

Of course, there is something to be said for the safety practitioners who focus on the minutia and lose sight of the real, serious risks. Safety professionals have to be quick-witted, nimble, and able to react to dynamic situations on a moment's notice. It's not easy and it's not fun, but if it was then they would charge admission instead of paying us.

So, thank you to all of you who tell me when my shoes are untied (I honestly couldn't care less but it's still nice for you to say so), thank you to all of you who bought this book; I hope you either really enjoy it and tell others to buy it, or even better hate it so much that you will organize book burnings. Book burnings sell books.

TABLE OF CONTENTS

CHAPTER 1

The View from The Outside In

There's a line from an episode of M*A*S*H where Frank Burns assumes temporary command of the camp. When Radar O'Reilly observes that "people aren't going to like that" in response to one of Frank's new directives. Frank tells Radar that "I didn't come here to be liked" to which Radar tells him "then you came to the right place." Sometimes that's how I feel working in safety. In other cases, I feel like The Far Side comic where a dog holding a violin sadly watching out the window while other dogs rapaciously attack a mailman.

I've always been the sort that if you don't want me in your clubhouse, I'll tear it down. Well, I probably won't tear it down, but if it gets blown down in a windstorm I will CLAIM I destroyed it, and you're just gullible to believe it.

This chapter is for all of those who feel that they have been left out of the good life

Safety: The View from The Outside In

I have always felt like an outsider in safety. When I worked in Organization Development or doing Lean Manufacturing implementations things made sense. People used science to make decisions and before a person made an assertion that person had to be prepared to defend that assertion with evidence, with facts. Then I went down the rabbit hole that was safety and met people who acted like they were pithed.

I never wanted to work in safety. Despite, or perhaps owing to, my father dying of mesothelioma, my brother-in-law being cut down in his prime from silicosis, my brother's friend dying after less than a month on the job, a friend of a friend who died at twenty when he fell in a vat of acid, and both grandfathers and a great uncle being killed on the job, I honestly didn't see it as being all that effectual, and if anything, I saw the safety people as being complicit in those deaths.

I also had my own negative experience with a quack doctor in the medical department at the factory in which I worked who was more concerned about getting people back on the line than in treating injuries. When I reported safety issues nothing happened, nobody responded, and the issues remained hazardous pieces of the jagged landscape that was my workplace. I had to fend for myself.

Later, as an organizational consultant, I met safety professionals who literally cared more about whether or not I tied my shoes and used the handrail than ensuring that no one died (which at least three did) on the job. These puffed up and sanctimonious boobs spent most of their time in their offices doing...well God knows what.

When I was offered the opportunity to interview with a firm that was working to make a company "the safest company in the world" I turned my friend and ex-coworker down flat. The safety professionals I had encountered were more interested in being seen as important than making the kind of structural changes required to become the safest company in the city let alone the world. No thank you, I was not interested in dealing with a bunch of change adverse people who were stuck in the position because they were politically connected but were as useless as the nipples on the tits of a ceramic bull.

Eventually, I relented, and the project was a huge success and much to my surprise I met safety professionals who were ambitious, hard-working, and smart. They actually CARED about people and when someone was seriously injured or killed they grieved and took to it to heart; all the while wondering what they could have done differently to have prevented the tragedy.

When the company and Union consented to allow my employer to create a similar offering for other customers, the Union lead on the project said, "I'm not going to play politics here. If it saves lives it should be shared."

So, for the next five years, I went on to work my magic and helped to transform companies from death traps to continuously improving companies who cared about safety.

But even though I could demonstrate case study after case study showing incredible improvements, it was a hard or even impossible sale to make. I had so many safety guys waste my time by having me come in only to brag about what a great job they were doing in safety. It felt like being invited to dinner and then being ambushed with a pitch to sell Amway.

Now I'm on the inside, and I can see many of the kinds of safety guys who killed my dad and brother-in-law; feckless bags of flesh who expend ten times the energy explaining why they can't do their jobs as they do trying to actually DO their jobs. To be sure, I've met many absolute superstar training professionals, but that's not the people who are shaping the view from the outside in.

The outsider's view of the safety guy is important because too often safety is seen as existing outside the business. The executives support the concept of safety without truly understanding it or owning responsibility for it. Middle managers continue to see the safety departments as the rat squad akin to the police department's Internal Affairs. Front-line supervisors are forced to please their bosses or the safety guy, and finally, the frontline workers see the safety practitioner as a schoolyard snitch, and we all know, "snitches end up in ditches".

This problem isn't going to go away until safety is so deeply integrated that it is no longer seen as external from Operations, and I am seeing some companies starting to get there, which is great, but in many others, the safety function is completely content to be the long-suffering victim; unappreciated and unwanted; the last kid picked for kickball.

An Open Letter to Safety Professionals from the 4,690 Workers Who Died on the Job in the United States in 2010

> I had just read another boastful post on an anti-social networking discussion group about how wonderful a job safety was doing. It made me think of my dad once a robust and powerful man reduces to skin and bones by mesiothema and my brother-in-law who bravely died of silicones. It made me angry that so many people just shrugged when it came to fatalities—they were quick to take credit for all the lives saved but no one wanted to be culpable for the workplace deaths. I decided to give the deceased workers a voice. It really angered a lot of people but in my opinion the ones most outraged were likely the most guilty.

Note: I thought long and hard about writing what you are about to read. Whenever I have taken issue with the self-congratulatory tone and self-righteous complacency that I see dangerously prevalent among safety professionals the ensuing storm of bile and abuse heaped on me has, at times, made me consider bagging it—stopping the blog, ending the speeches, and retiring from my gigs as a safety columnist. But after more than a decade of decline, the workplace death toll in the U.S. has risen. In 2010, while some of you were jetting off to Brazil on your citizen diplomat boondoggle an average of 13 workers died a day. If you get offended by the truth; stop reading. If you do read on, save us both time and aggravation and spare me your outraged venomous hate mail, I don't want to hear it and all it does is convince me of the veracity of my message. What follows is perhaps my magnum opus of provocative work. I dedicate it to my father who died of mesothelioma, my brother-in-law who died of silicosis after working for decades on Zug Island, once listed in the Guinness Book of World Records as the dirtiest square mile on the planet Earth, my brother who suffered permanent memory loss after an industrial accident, my many friends who died in industrial accidents but most especially to those who have taken such extraordinary measures to try attack and insult me in an effort to silence my message.

Dear Safety Guy:

I hope you are doing well and are enjoying this lovely weather with family and friends. I don't want to harsh your buzz or bust up the barbecue, but I died in the workplace this week and I want you to know that I am deeply disappointed in you. You see, I trusted you and you failed me. And not just me, 12 other guys died alongside me and 13 of us died yesterday, and another 13 tomorrow, in fact, every day; day in and day out. 4,690 of us in all…wait that's not quite right another 50,000 or so died from illnesses caused by working waist deep in poisons or breathing in chemicals that would kill us slowly, horribly.

Some of us died because we did stupid things, some of us weren't adequately trained, some of us underestimated the dangers we faced, and some of us overestimated our skills, but none of us expected to die. None of us reported for work expecting to get killed. None of our lives were any less valuable than yours and before you get all self-righteous it wasn't my job not to die, it was YOUR job to make sure my job didn't kill me. But I DID die, and I doubt you will even get a verbal warning.

As I write this I can see you squirm. Does it make you uncomfortable for me to hold you accountable? Is it unfair that I blame you for something that I did that killed me? After all, how—you ask—can I hold you accountable for my own stupidity? You didn't tell me to do the things that I did today that ultimately got me killed. But it was your job to keep me alive. I certainly didn't do those things that I did because I wanted more butt time (as I've heard you describe to your colleagues at conferences or huddled around a coffee talking about how stupid we all are). I screwed up, and that screw up got me killed. Everyone makes mistakes, but nobody should have to die because of a mistake made at work. I counted on you to anticipate and correct the things that would kill me before I got hurt; where were you when I died?

I really liked the safety BINGO, and I sure loved the extra money when we got as a bonus for zero injury days. Were you too stupid to know that these things created an environment where we were essentially bribed to stay quiet about injuries? Or did you just recklessly disregard the fact that you were creating incident statistics that lulled the decision makers into a false sense of security regarding our risk level? I knew what you were doing was wrong, but I wasn't about to turn the whole company against me and speak up. Congratulations on having such a great safety record; how does my death look on your resume?

I can only imagine how disappointed you were to learn that worker fatalities in the U.S. have spiked—I think we all figured that when we sourced all that the really dangerous work out to the Third World that we were home free. I feel kind of bad about it now—the afterlife is full Third World workers who bought it because their lives were thought to be so much cheaper than mine. It turns out they weren't that much different from me. They had families who loved them, wives and children who counted on them. All they wanted to do was go to work, make a buck, and come home safe. They had lives snatched away from them the same as me; just because we showed up for work.

I know that as you read this you are tempted to excuse yourself and tell yourself that my death isn't your fault. That management put profits before safety; that the Union shut down what you wanted to do; that you can't protect people when they won't listen to you, and all that other crap I've heard you say a thousand times. Stop feeling sorry for yourself; you aren't the victim here. Before you blame management... the last time I checked most of you ARE management. The same goes for leadership— isn't that what you are supposed to be, a leader? If a juggler can't do his job guess what? he drops a couple of balls; no harm, no foul. If YOU are incompetent, people DIE; I DIED. 4,695 other people died. If you can't hack it, get out of the game. Stop worrying about the condition of your 401K and retire or change careers; become a florist, that way the only thing at risk of dying because of your ineptitude is a dozen carnations.

Remember how much we all enjoyed your children's safety poster contest? Now it just seems sad. How about all those pictures of people doing unsafe things? Remember how we'd laugh about how stupid they were? somehow, it's just not that funny anymore. Did you really think you were making a difference with that crap?

Think I'm being too hard on you? Think you deserve some credit for doing your best? Screw you, I can get a baboon in here to do its best. Your best doesn't measure up. Your best got people killed. And I don't believe for a second that you were doing your best when I died. It's not like you weren't warned. When people post things on blogs or magazines that were critical of your profession you chose to get indignant and hammered out a "how dare you insult the hard-working men and women of the august profession of worker health and safety blah blah blah", you remember that don't you? It was a hell of a lot easier to write an indignant email telling your peers to tell that guy to shut up than it was to consider for one microsecond that you might have to do something different. And now even in the face of my death, you are still too arrogant to consider that there might be a better way.

Was it the culture that killed me? Did you see all the signs that we were ripe for a fatality? Did you storm around the office saying if someone doesn't do something that someone was going to die? Did "you tell the bastards"? Well if you continued to take a paycheck in a hopeless environment where leaders didn't care about the safety of the workers I decry you as a craven and fool.

I know you see yourself as underappreciated and doing a thankless job. Well, I'm dead and thanks for nothing. You aren't a hero; you don't even deserve a footnote in my obituary. You get no thanks because there is nothing you've done that deserves the smallest modicum of gratitude.

Before you wrap yourself in the blanket of "there was no way I could have prevented his death" there are plenty of people working for change and we NEED change. These people work against impossible odds against people just like you. You have a decision: you can either be on the side of change or be part of the forces lined up against it. You can either save lives or save your twisted sense of self-righteousness; you choose, and for the first time in your life be prepared to live with the consequences of your choices; I doubt you have that in you. So, what now? My role in this argument ends at the grave. What will you do next? Between now and Monday, 26 more workers will die in the U.S. and ten times that worldwide. Will it just be a statistic? Will it be a shame? What will you do differently in response to my death? Do you care even a little bit? Are you more concerned about saving lives or saving your own ass?

Sincerely,

4,695 dead workers and counting

What's Wrong With Safety Training . . . And How To Fix It

Illustration by Brett Radlicki

http://www.fabricatingandmetalworking.com/2011/12/whats-wrong-with-safety-training-and-how-to-fix-it/ **Reprinted with permission.**

This is how it all began (well not counting my writing for the now defunct Flat Rock Guardian (a weekly newspaper for which I was a community stringer and columnist. The editor of Fabricating and Metalworking, Mike Riley, discovered this white paper on my company's webpage and decided to run it as an article. That was all the nudge I needed for a multi-year run as a contributing editor.

It's five minutes past the start of your training course and three-quarters of the class still hasn't arrived. Those participants that showed up on time fidget in their seats and look impatiently at their watches. Somebody runs to a phone and 15 minutes later you finally get started to a class a third of the size it should be. Sound familiar?

Let's face it, many companies do a poor job of safety training, the participants rarely retain or apply the things they learn, and except for complying with government regulations little is accomplished. Safety training is required to protect workers so why should we have to fight with people to get them to complete the training?

The most common reasons given for resisting safety training include: the training is boring, the material is common sense or doesn't pertain to me, and we only do it because we are made to go – not because we expect to learn anything useful.

Safety training boring? How could anyone say such heresy? Well, the reality is that most people are turned off by someone reading off PowerPoint slides that literally contain a government regulation. And as for the training not containing information that applies to them, I challenge participants to find a safety topic that doesn't apply to them.

Years ago, I worked seasonal help delivering packages for a postal delivery company. I had a one-hour course on lifting and carrying packages. Now given that I would only be working a maximum of six weeks and would not likely be pursuing this work as a career, it would have been easy enough for me to dismiss the class as pointless compliance. Instead, I was surprised to learn useful skills that I remember and use to this day. What was the difference between this course and the hundreds of safety courses I've been made to endure over the years?

Simple. This course was effectively designed and expertly delivered and, believe it or not, you can do the same with your safety courses by following some basic rules:

RULE 1: WRITE GOOD OBJECTIVES

Good course objectives are like a checklist of the topics you want to cover, and the more time you spend writing strong objectives the easier it is to write the rest of your course. When writing course objectives ask yourself two questions: "What do I want the participants to be able to 'do' when they leave my training course?" and "How will I know that the participants are able to do the things I presented?"

Being the astute reader that you are, you undoubtedly noticed that I said "do" (it helps that I put the word in quotes) and not "know". The best objectives are measurable and observable behaviors, and while it's pretty easy to measure what someone can and cannot do, it's darn near impossible to tell what someone knows, unless there's an accompanying observable behavior.

In broad strokes, when we talk about imparting knowledge we are talking about "education" and when we talk about teaching a skill we are talking about "training". Let's put it this way, you may be in favor of your fifth grader getting sex education, but probably wouldn't be crazy about him or her getting sex *training*. Every good instructional objective will have three elements:

1. Identification of the skill expressed using action verbs

2. Criteria for success

3. Measurement parameters

Identification of a skill using action verbs may seem fairly obvious to you, but when you sit down with pen and paper and try to write an objective that clearly identifies the skills you want to impart, it can get difficult, even frustrating.

Action verbs denote a person doing something, which is important when you are trying to provide skills training because when you train someone, you really want them to DO something. So, when you write an objective it's crucial that you use an action verb to describe what you want the participants to be able to do. The table below is far from an exhaustive list, but it's a good place to start:

Action Verbs	Passive Verbs
Describe	Understand
List	Know
Compare	Value
Contrast	Be Aware of (okay I cheated but you
Cite	get my point)
Explain	
Calculate	
Determine	

Establishing a criteria for success also SEEMS easy, but can be even more difficult than describing the skill, but once you've determined what actions the participants will be able to perform you need to identify how good is "good enough". The perfectionists among you will demand 100 percent and that's laudable, but it also sets up an unrealistic expectation and the likelihood that you will end up retraining a boat load of participants who will never pass with 100 percent accuracy.

I like to use the 90-90-90 rule. This rule holds that the course will be judged effective when 90 percent of the participants are able to demonstrate 90 percent of the skills with 90 percent accuracy. And as good as this rule is, it's a stretch for a lot of courses, but it's still a nice target, and when we are doing safety training, I really think it allows us to set the bar a little higher than we might ordinarily.

Okay, so now you've decided what you want the participants to do, and how well they have to do it, you must establish some way to evaluate how "good" is "good enough", and for that we need clear measurement parameters. Defining measurement parameters can be a lot trickier than it appears at first blush.

Let's say you're putting together a course in Right to Know and you've decided that you want the participants to be able to understand their specific legal rights. It's impossible to observe a person's "understanding" and so you will need to write an objective that identifies behaviors that you can observe but that also demonstrate an understanding of the content. Using our action verbs, you might write something like:

> After completing this course, the participant will be able to list the seven legal rights pertaining to his or her right to be informed of the hazards to which he or she might be exposed while in the workplace, in ten minutes with 90% accuracy

RULE 2: FOLLOW A SIMPLE COURSE DESIGN MODEL

If people think safety training are boring, then they haven't talked to a lot of Instructional Designers. These clods will bury you in hours of jargon and complex models largely developed by academics for academics, but if you listen closely and are able to stay awake long enough, you just might find that some of the things they are telling you are worthwhile.

I've taught many Train-the-Trainer workshops where the participants follow a simplified course development model that seems to work pretty well for subject matter experts who are pressed into doing training. The model I teach in these sessions is simple ("it" refers to a skill you are trying to teach):

1. Introduce it. Adults need to understand why they should learn the skill you are trying to teach, and believe that learning this skill has something meaningful and valuable in it for them. When you introduce a skill quickly and convincingly let the audience know the WIFM ("what's in it for me?")

2. **Define it.** When you define the skill, be specific about exactly what the skill is, and—where appropriate—is not.

3. **Explain it.** Once you have defined the skill, you need to explain the context in which the person will use the skill, and provide the participants with criteria so they can judge whether or not they are correctly applying the skill. Far too often skills are defined in such vague terms that the participants don't know what they are expected to learn.

4. Illustrate it. Using examples, visual aids, or other means, illustrate what the skill looks like when being properly applied. Here is where drawing on your experience and telling war-stories can help you to get the point across. You can also share how you came to understand a concept or tricks that you used while learning a skill.

5. Demonstrate it. Demonstrating a skill is crucial, both in building a skill and maintaining your credibility. Demonstrating a skill allows the participant to see how the skill is correctly performed and can ask questions to clarify things that they may not understand.

6. Allow people to practice it. Once people have seen the skill, they are ready to try it themselves. While they practice the skill, you should be providing guidance and coaching so that people are able to refine the newly acquired skill in the safety of a supervised situation.

7. Evaluate it. If you wrote a good objective, evaluating the participant's progress should be very easy, all you need do is to compare the participant's demonstration of the skill with the criteria for success you established in the objective.

Remember: not everyone will be successful the first time they try to demonstrate the skill. As a successful safety instructor, you must repeat the demonstration and practice steps until you are satisfied that the individual is able to correctly demonstrate the skill.

By following these seven steps for each of your topics you should be able to effectively build the skills that you are supposed to be teaching, of course designing a course around these simple steps is a lot harder to do than it first appears.

Now some of you are probably thinking, "yeah right, sounds good on paper, but those steps really can't be applied in a Health and Safety training course. Okay, let's say you're teaching a course in "Right to Know" or "Hazard Communication" and you have written an objective something like this:

> In ten minutes and given a sample MSDS the participants will be able to: read the sheet and determine the ingredients, proper handling requirements, reactivity and flammability of a substance and the necessary emergency response to accidental exposure to the substance, with 90% accuracy.

For our first step, introducing the topic you might say something like," a Material Safety Data Sheet is a document that contains important information about the characteristics and actual or potential hazards of a substance."

You might describe it a by saying "Material Safety Data Sheets are often referred to simply as an MSDS and they identify the manufacturer of the substance (with name, address, phone, and fax number). MSDS sheets typically include (1) chemical identity, (2) hazardous ingredients, (3) physical and chemical properties, (4) fire and explosion data, (5) reactivity data, (6) health hazards data, (7) exposure limits data, (8) precautions for safe storage and handling, (9) need for protective gear, and (10) spill control, cleanup, and disposal procedures. You need to be able to read and interpret an MSDS, so you know what measures you will need to take to protect yourself from the hazards associated with working with the substance."

A nice way to illustrate the importance of being able to read an MSDS is to pull a spray bottle half filled with iced tea and ask for a volunteer to drink it. When no one volunteers, ask the group why. The most likely responses will center around not knowing what the substance in the spray bottle is, or what potential harm it may do to someone who drinks it.

You can easily demonstrate the skill using an oversized MSDS as a visual aid. I recommend not using an overhead projection, just because I like to vary the media and methods to better hold the attention of the participants. Using the oversized MSDS you can read to MSDS to the class pointing out where each bit of information is located on the visual aid.

Using a second oversized MSDS you can then ask participants to answer questions about the substance that is described on the sheet and evaluate their responses. Once you are satisfied that each participant is able to demonstrate the skills to your satisfaction you have successfully achieved your instructional objective.

RULE 3: KEEP THE LEARNERS ENGAGED

Far too many safety courses focus on content and ignore delivery. Instructors drone on and on oblivious to a room full of participants who have completely checked out mentally. A good safety course should keep the learners engaged by employing some simple instructional methods.

Estimates of the average attention span of an adult American range between 10 and 15 minutes. That may seem hard to believe until you think about the way the brain works. Our brains take in information for about 30 seconds and then spend about a minute and a half processing the information. This cycle continues until the brain feels the stress of concentration and moves on to a new subject.

The times I use are purely to illustrate the dynamic, and the fact checker for this article should recognize that the veracity of the exact timing has the veracity of a poorly researched Wikipedia article or your average doom and gloom email warning.

Irrespective of the exact timing of this processing, if an instructor throws too much information at an individual too quickly, the brain simply can't keep up and shuts down. Conversely, if the brain receives information too slowly, the mind tends to wander and seek out other input to process; a phenomenon is commonly called *daydreaming*.

There are ways with which you can hold people's attention longer. First, vary your delivery methods. Many safety instructors have one delivery method: lecture. Lecture is very useful and widely used in traditional education and it certainly has a place in safety training, but it shouldn't be the only method an instructor uses.

Lectures are popular among safety instructors because people tend to model the methods most familiar to them, and since most safety instructors sat through numerous lectures in college, they gravitate to this delivery method. A ten-minute lecture that introduces defines and explains a topic is an excellent way to provide the participants with a lot of information quickly, but then a good instructor should use another delivery method to illustrate the point.

I like to use question-and-answer or a group discussion to illustrate the skills I am trying to teach, but you might also consider a case study, a video, or a simulation exercise to illustrate. I prefer to save case studies and simulation exercises for the demonstration and practice steps of the instructional process.

A case study is typically an in-depth examination of one specific situation that is representative of the circumstances under which the learners will apply the skill. A good case study should have a dilemma that the reader is asked to solve. When you write a case study, be sure you provide enough information, so the participants can draw correct conclusions but don't provide so much information that the solution to the problem is obvious.

Writing a good case study is similar to writing anything worth reading — you have to keep the reader interested and engaged — except that case studies differ from written descriptions in that case studies are designed to teach a lesson of some sort. But a well written case study is only part of what makes the tool valuable.

How you facilitate a case study is at least as important as how well the case study is written. While case studies can be used as part of individual or group work, I prefer dividing the class into small groups and having the participants engage in discussion. When facilitating a case study have the participants in each group read the case and discuss the questions you've either included in your handouts or posted in the room. (You don't want to just pose the questions unless you want to have to keep repeating the questions to throughout the exercise.)

Once each group has discussed the questions and arrived at a consensus have a group spokesperson share their responses with the entire class. The discussion of the case study in the entire group will allow you to gage the participants understanding of the points you'd hope to make by using the case study.

When it comes to evaluation there's no substitute for a good experiential exercise (or simulation). An experiential exercise/simulation is a controlled environment where the learner can perform the skills without exposing themselves to real-life dangers that might be associated with performing the skills under the actual conditions that the participants will ultimately be expected to perform the skill.

Years ago, I worked as a security guard in a nuclear power plant. You can imagine how important safety was and can probably understand how much safety training we had to compete. One course was on the PPE associated with entering a radioactive area. Obviously, the instructor couldn't take us into an actual radioactive area for training. The situation was even more complicated because while there were over 25 participants, there was only two sets of PPE available.

Despite these challenges the instructor managed to train us in the procedure for putting on the gear and taking it off. The instructor accomplished his objective by using a simple simulation. The instructor took us to an adjacent room where he had used masking tape to mark an area as "Radioactive", he instructed us to (in pairs) demonstrate the proper procedure for putting on our imaginary gear, and then removing the gear.

The procedure for doing so was painfully specific with each piece of gear needed to be put on in a specific order. If while removing the gear we made a mistake, he would say, "congratulations, you are radioactive" and tell the offending participant to go to the end of the line. I still remember how much fun we had, but more importantly, 20 years later, I still remember how to don and remove a radiation suit! The exercise was more than just engaging, it was meaningful and effective.

RULE 4: SETUP AND DEBRIEF YOUR EXERCISES

"Okay, I'm gonna show a video" is typically training-speak for "nap time". Remember the only reason we do ANYTHING in a training course is in support of a corresponding objective, so whenever you present a topic you need to set it up and debrief it. Let's take that video for example, why are we showing it? What objective does viewing the video accomplish? Why should I as a participant watch the video?

If you don't have answers to these questions, then you probably shouldn't be using video. When you set up an activity begin with the objective you hope to achieve. For example, if you are showing a video about confined space entry, you might introduce the video by saying, "we're going to watch a short video on confined space entry. I think this video does a particularly nice job demonstrating the correct procedure for entering a confined space. A little later in the course we will be practicing entering a simulated confined space, so you may want to pay particular attention to that portion of the video."

After the exercise it is crucial that you debrief. A debrief is a way of deepening the participants understanding of the point you are making and helps them to retain the skill longer. When you debrief make sure you focus on the lesson that you want the participant to take away from the activity. A good debrief should encourage participants to interpret the exercise and to analyze what they have learned. I like to start with an open-ended question like, "what did you think of the video?"

The problem with a question like that is you are likely to get an emotional response like, "I didn't like it" or "It was stupid". Or you might get someone who critiques the production values. While these responses may not seem appropriate to our purposes, it allows the participants to get those feelings off their chest so that you can talk about more substantive topics. I like to follow with another open question like, "what did you learn from the video?"

Unless you ask the first question (what did you think of the video?) you are likely to get answers like "nothing". It's not that people will always react negatively to your activities, but allowing a vent question will relieve the stress of the people that DID react badly. If the group seems to have missed the point, you can gently steer the group back toward the concepts you want them to take away from the exercise.

RULE 5: DO TRAINING TO PROVIDE SKILLS, NOT MERELY ACHIEVE COMPLIANCE

A lot of safety training is seen as a necessary evil by the organization and major a pain in the butt by the individual. How can you ever train people who honestly and ardently believe that they aren't attending your training, they're being subjected to it.

But we have to do safety training to comply with the law! We don't have a choice; we have to present it and people have to attend it. While compliance is certainly an important part of why we do training, it MUST be secondary to protecting workers. There can never be a tradeoff between imparting skills necessary for workers to be safe and complying with a regulation.

Before accepting my current position, I spent many years as head of training for a large, international manufacturer. Because we had locations in Asia, Europe, and throughout North America we were beset by varied and sometimes contradictory compliance requirements. In addition to governments, the executives over our operating units had training courses that they would decide were mandatory for ALL EMPLOYEES.

It was often tough, because I would disagree that the part time receptionist at a plant in Montreal would need 16 hours of Problem Solving training, and yet, that was the requirement. I finally realized that compliance was not the anathema of skill building, and in fact, with a little thought compliance can be your friend.

Never tell an adult that the reason they are in your safety training is because the law says they have to be. That may well be an accurate statement, but it sets a tone where the participants are being treated as convicts or children.

Take Hazard Communication training. Haz Com used to be, for me, the symbol of pointless compliance training. I believed that we did it yearly, not because it was necessary, or valuable, but plain and simply because the law said we had to, and if we didn't we risked a big fine. Can you imagine how effective I was teaching a topic that I was just presenting because I had too? How receptive do you think the adults who were dragged into the class against their will were to the course?

The evaluations of the course accurately derided the training as a waste of time. Having such a fragile psyche, I really took the criticism to heart and decide to do something about it. I sat down and did some soul searching, and when I started to focus on the skills I wanted the participants to learn, instead of the compliance box I was going to check, I was able to make some significant and important improvements to the course.

I started by asking why OSHA required the course. I reasoned that the course was probably required because people were getting injured because they inadvertently exposed themselves to hazards, and did so because their employers — either out of ignorance, maliciousness, or negligence — never warned them of the dangers. This realization helped me to retool the course to meet the goal of warning people about dangers in the workplace and informing them of their rights under the law instead of merely checking the box. Overnight the participants got more excited, did better on the posttests, and were more involved in the course.

For my part, I enjoyed presenting the course and felt the time I spent was worthwhile.

RULE 6: STAY FOCUSED ON THE *NEED* TO KNOW AND GET RID OF THE *NICE TO*

A fair amount of safety training was developed by Subject Matter Experts (SMEs) and SMEs often have difficulty separating the "need to know" from the "nice to know". Many SMEs are convinced that a skill can only be required once an individual fully grasps the scientific principles behind the skills and has a complete understanding of the topic presented.

These courses bog down in technical minutiae that does nothing to increase the proficiency with which the participants will apply the skills being taught. I once worked with an engineer to develop a course on the operation and maintenance of a machine that made magnets. The engineer insisted on an 8-hour course that covered every conceivable element in the magnetizing of strontium ferrite.

The engineer insisted that the participants learned all the fine points of magnetism, the physical and chemical properties of strontium ferrite, how compounds and alloys are made, and a host of other information that had no direct connection with the operation of the machine. So much information was shared in this course, that many participants could not perform the four skills associated with operating the magnetizer.

RULE 7: OPEN WITH AN INTRODUCTION AND CLOSE WITH A SUMMARY

Like any good presentation, a good safety course follows the simple structure of (a) tell them what you hope to accomplish and why they should listen to you, (b) tell them and (c) tell them what you have told them.

There are five elements of an introduction:

1. Housekeeping. Housekeeping is a catch-all phrase for basic information that doesn't really fit neatly into any other category. It's important that you model the behaviors that you expect from the participants, so you should always start a safety course with safety information, like emergency evacuation procedures or similar information.

When sharing the housekeeping information don't take it for granted that people will know where the restrooms are, how long the course is, and if breaks will be provided. Be sure to get the participants to sign the sign-in sheet, and in many workplaces, housekeeping may include a pre-evaluation of some sort.

2. WIIFM. I've already mentioned how important it is for adults to understand the WIIFM — "What's in It for Me?" but it's important enough to briefly revisit. To be truly effective, a training course must provide irrefutable value to the participants. The participants are asked to sacrifice their time and attention and they need to know up front what benefits they will derive from this sacrifice. If the participants don't find the WIIFM particularly compelling they are likely to leave the session, if not physically than mentally.

3. Establishing Expertise. Almost as important as the WIIFM is the speaker's credibility. Subconsciously (if not consciously) the participants in your class are wondering why they should listen to you; specifically, what makes you such a darned expert?

Until you establish your credibility on the topic you are presenting many in the audience will check out and stop listening. You needn't go to extremes to demonstrate your expertise, but a short explanation of your background and familiarity with the topic will go a long way to getting people to listen to what you have to say. You should keep your explanation of your background short but be clear and specific— as hard to believe as this may seem not everyone in the world knows what a CSP is or what being one has to do with lock out!

4. Establishing Expectations. A good introduction will quickly and definitively establish the participants' expectations of the course. The simplest way to establish expectations is to cover the objectives. Many instructors will read the objectives to the participants quickly and without comment; this is a mistake.

In addition to being the blueprint for your course design, the course objectives are an important part of establishing expectations, both by what they say and in how they are presented. Instructors who rush through, dance around, or skip over the objectives non-verbally convey that the objectives really aren't all that important. So instead of seeing the slide with objectives as a necessary evil, take some quality time and explain not only the objective, but WHY it's an objective as well.

5. Ice Breaker. I have a love-hate relationship with icebreakers. An icebreaker is intended to relax the participants, help to further establish expectations, and transition from the introduction to the main body of your course. A good icebreaker can prove a point so strongly that the participants will take it with them and retain it for years.

A good icebreaker can also provide a shared experience that can become the foundation of the course and a useful reference point. Poor icebreakers (and man, have I seen plenty of them) waste time, come off as cutsie and dumb, and turn off the participants. The difference between good and bad icebreakers is in the course design.

To design a good icebreaker, take a look at your course goal (which is really the common theme of your objectives) and work backward. What short, attention getting, and impactful activity can you use to drive home the point of your course?

Years ago, I learned to juggle and have used juggling as an icebreaker. In fact, truth be told I've probably over used juggling. Why use juggling? Well, first of all, it's not because I can, nor is because I made an impulse buy years ago and spent $10 on three bean-bag juggling toucans, although you have to admit those are pretty compelling reasons. No, I like to use juggling because it: is a highly active activity, is a highly visible activity, is entertaining for the participants to watch, builds tension and anticipation, and it's a metaphor for many of the skills that I thought from time management to importance of training.

You can use a wide range of activities as icebreakers, but unless you debrief the icebreaker and demonstrate a credible point, people will see it as a waste of time, irrespective of how enjoyable it was. Whenever I selected juggling as an icebreaker I started with a point I wanted to make and found that juggling made that point particularly well. I never started with the idea of juggling and tried to force fit a point or metaphor.

Closing your presentation with a summary is also important. A summary ties the course together and give you with one last chance to drive home those important points. There are four elements to an effective summary:

1. Review. A review is a quick overview that reminds the participants what has been covered in the course. A review is useful in establishing parity between the topics and lets the participants know that each topic was equally important. A review also transitions the participants' attention toward the course conclusion. Without an effective review the course feels truncated and the participants feel as if the instructor ran out of time and didn't adequately cover the material (even if the participant thoroughly covered each point.)

2. Call to Action. Throughout the course you've been reinforcing the importance of the topics presented and the how they will be used, now, using a call to action you need to sum up in a sentence or two (max!) what you want them to do with the skills you have taught them. A call to action could be as simple as "I want you to get out there and work safely."

3. Conclusion. A conclusion is different from a review, in that the conclusion is a subtle announcement that the course is winding down and that the participants will soon be free to leave. Keep your conclusions short, but while concluding your course be sure to thank the participants for their time and attention.

4. Post Evaluation. Most of us work in places where at least some form of course evaluation is required, so be sure you have your participants complete all the necessary forms — post tests, course evaluation sheets, and the sign in sheet — before they bolt out of your classroom like a prison break.

RULE 8: EVALUATE YOUR EFFECTIVENESS AND IMPROVE

Safety is a dynamic topic and fortunately for us, it is typically revisited yearly. Always evaluate the effectiveness of your course (ideally through formal pre-and posttests, but if that isn't an option then using informal, observational evaluations) and the effectiveness of your presentation. At least once a year evaluate the content to ensure that it is still current and complete.

Most people will probably never look forward to safety training, but by following these 8 rules, you can ensure that people won't dread coming to your course. And who knows? as word gets around that your training courses are focused on skills building, are entertaining and interesting, keep the participants attention, and provided at least some useful information you might just find that people show up on time, turn off their cell phones, participate, and make your time together more worthwhile.

FOUR REASONS, EIGHT LESSONS

(Originally published in <u>Facility Safety Management</u> April 2011. Used with permission.

> Conventional wisdom holds that people won't report near misses because they fear repercussions associated with admitting that they screwed up, but in most cases, conventional wisdom is wrong.

Near misses — incidents where no one was seriously injured but COULD have been — provide us with an opportunity to learn about system failures and correct the hazards before a catastrophic incident happens. But people are reticent to report these mishaps, and organizations lose this opportunity. Why? Many, if not most safety professionals land on "people are afraid they'll get in trouble," and while this is sometimes the case, more often it's not.

In the past two weeks, I've been involved with three near misses that I did not report. Why? Was I afraid? What was it about these incidents that made me balk at reporting them?

In each case I did nothing wrong. In the first case, I was trying to turn off a light in a cubicle and as I felt along the bottom of the light to locate the power switch, I instead crammed my palm into the plastic light cover; it hurt, but it didn't injure me. Had I been hurrying or had the plastic been jagged I could have been injured—from a safety standpoint I could have been cut, burned or received an electrical shock.

The second near miss was a slip on the snow walking down concrete steps into a traffic area. I slipped but managed to grab the handrail and while I was off-balance I didn't fall; so, another near miss.

I did a quick analysis and again, I was blameless. I wasn't walking too fast, I was wearing appropriate footwear, and I was walking in an area intended for pedestrians. The steps were sloped down and forward and being concrete and smooth, the slightest moisture (never mind ice and snow) can easily cause a loss of traction. To further complicate things, there are no sidewalks from this parking lot to the entrance forcing people to walk on the snow-covered grass or in traffic. Not only is an injury probable, but if an injury does occur, the incident promises to be severe or even fatal.

The third near miss involved me catching the heel of my shoe on a step and falling forward. In this case, I was also able to catch myself using the rail and felt only mild discomfort in my knee and ankle. Things most certainly could have been much worse, but I was lucky. In this case, as with the others, I was not distracted, I was following procedures, and I was not behaving unsafely.

But, I didn't report any of these near misses and here's why:

After the first incident, I asked a colleague if the organization had a near miss reporting process. She asked me what that was. Clearly, my safety jargon was getting in the way, so I asked her differently, "how do we report injuries?" She explained that there was a system, but she didn't know what it was and that I should ask the department head. Reason number 1: reporting a near miss is hard.

When I asked the head of the department about near miss reporting I got the same general response: I don't know. When she asked me why I was inquiring, not in an accusatory tone, but in more of a concerned, "Did you want to report something?" sort of way, I found myself dismissing the near miss as too trivial to report (when was the last time somebody died looking for a light switch?) Reason number 2: Because there wasn't any serious, consequence resulting from the near miss, it wasn't worth reporting.

After my near slip on the ice, I noticed a group of people talking about the fact that the lack of sidewalks meant that they had to walk into traffic and that the few sidewalks that did exist were slick with ice. I shared my experience with the icy steps, and one person responded, if you call facilities they tell you that you have to fill out a work order and even when you do, they don't do anything. Reason number 3: Because people believe, the organization does not value the information.

By the time I caught my heel on the step and almost fell, I was fully indoctrinated into a culture that did not report near misses, but I desperately wanted to avoid being one of those people that ignored the problem. I mentally resolved to find the process and report these near misses. Then I mentally walked myself through the scenario of me reporting these three near misses and decided that I would look like: a) an accident-prone klutz, b) I would be seen as Chicken Little and c) nothing would be done with the information anyway. Reason 4: The risk to reward ratio is stacked against anyone who reports a near miss.

For the record, this organization has an amazingly nurturing and employee centric culture. Employee development is encouraged and training is a key priority. And yet I was clearly and quickly "told" that near miss reporting was not a priority, not valued, and the organization was not concerned with my safety, despite none of these things being true.

So, what did I take away? Several things:

People feel foolish when they do something that results in a near miss even if they did nothing wrong, and people who feel foolish are unlikely to advertise it.

People will only report a near miss if it is easy to do so, and ideally, if doing so is anonymous. Advertising the process is key.

If an organization solicits people to report, hazards or near misses it had better be ready to respond quickly and effectively to the hazard.

Even a veteran safety professional is not immune to peer pressure.

The fear of being made to look like a whiner or a wimp is greater than the desire to improve the safety of the workplace.

You absolutely must have a blame-free reporting process. If I was reluctant to report something that happened for which I was in no way responsible, how much more reluctant will I be for an incident where my behavior played a role in causing the incident?

My guess is that near miss reporting will most likely only happen in cases where it is virtually impossible not to report it. This needs to change but unless near miss reporting is given the same priority as reporting a serious injury, we are doomed to a world of ignorance.

We get what we measure. Nobody seemed very interested in collecting my information, so I was certainly not going to push it.

Sadly, while we preach a good fight when it comes to near miss reporting, we don't do a good job in executing because many of us start with the assumption that people won't report near misses because they are afraid. Until we move beyond that mindset, our organizations will be at risk and we will continue to underestimate our risk of serious injuries and fatalities.

CHAPTER 2

Readers' Choice

My writing inspires strong emotions—typically it's either loved or detested, so when my publisher told me to pick 20 or 30 or my best posts (out of a total of 853) sufficed to say it wasn't quite so simple. Also, once when some of my magazine publishers gave their permission to use articles I had written for them it became impossible for a lazy man such as myself to choose. So, I threw the question out to my readers and literally within moments I had enough suggestions to fill five books. So, in gratitude to those who made suggestions I dedicate this chapter to you.

SPITTING ON FOREST FIRES

My battle for the safety of my neighborhood continues. One would think that my request that heavy equipment stop plowing through stop signs at 20+ mph adjacent to a popular park would be a no brainer, and in a way, it is. The people involved seem to have no brains at all. This has got my brain twisting and turning with questions. Why do otherwise reasonable people fail to see the risk endemic to this situation? Why do people defend their reckless behavior in an environment where there is most certainly not going to be any meaningful consequence? Beyond the questions it's got me thinking about courage and cowardice.

I don't ask for much from the readers of my blog, but I am going to ask you to indulge me a bit this week as I meander away from the edge of the topic of WORKER safety and into the world of safety as a whole.

You see I met some friends at my local watering hole. It's a faux Irish bar with the only real irritants being the occasional Journey or country music song on the jukebox and me of course. It's a largely homogeneous crowd where everyone looks like they belong there. You might get the occasional stranger from the Elk's lodge across the street, but for all intents and purposes you can tell who's there for a drink and who is up to no good.

Into that mix, a couple of minutes apart walked two parties, an aging drug addict (believe me having an ex-wife who died of a drug overdose after a decades long downward spiral) accompanied by a young girl of about 11 or 12. They sat at the bar looking like a turd in a punchbowl, and immediately caught my eye. The bar was crowded and the people who ordinarily would have quickly interceded were too busy to notice. About five minutes later, a man who looked like someone had sent down to central casting for a child molester came in and sat next to them. The adults chatted in conspiratorial tones and the woman and child moved to a table near the door. The man kept manufacturing reasons to go to the door, each time stopping to chat briefly while looking around to see if a bouncer, or cop, or for all I know a rhinoceros. This went on for 10 minutes or so. I brought it to the the bar owners attention and she said she was monitoring the situation, but I knew she was just too busy to do much about it. Soon the woman and child left. Moments later the man got up and followed and I was tight on his tail. When I went outside I saw the woman and the man negotiating something, so I walked up and asked flat out if there needed to be some police involvement. "In what?!?!" The man screamed in alarm. I told him I would let them suss that out. Then I did something that I did often. I took his picture and those of his companions. The man nervously asked what I was going to do with that and I said, "well that depends on how all this turns out." They quickly went their separate ways.

Was the safety of that young girl my responsibility? Did I do anything but forestall the inevitable? Should I have left it to the police? I don't know. But I do know this: intervening isn't easy, and most people won't thank you, especially if you point out that what they are doing is wrong. But not intervening is cowardice, and I have always been too quick with my mouth and my fists. I've learned better ways, and that as one coworker once said of me (referring to the staggering amount of work that I am able to produce in such a short time) that I cannot hold people to the same standard I hold myself to.

Recently I met a safety leader and truly remarkable thinker who turned me on to the Hummingbird Effect but in a simplified form that could be applied to safety. Now bear with me because I am creating this from memory as I can't find the original text. Here is a link to a version https://www.youtube.com/watch?v=A42Cp_RUJdQ

The crux of the story is this: The animals of the forest are awakened to a fire that was raging out of control and threatening to consume their home. They all fled to safety and stood idly by as the only home they had known their whole life was engulfed in a fiery holocaust. At some point they noticed that a hummingbird was flying from the lake and take a mouthful of water and flying to the fire and spitting the water onto the flames. The other animals were incredulous and asked the hummingbird what it hoped to accomplish; that its efforts were too little and could not possible work. The exhausted hummingbird said, "I'm doing the best that I can." The other animals, perhaps shamed at their own reluctance joined in the effort and ultimately extinguished the flames.

I thought back on this story as I contemplated the what ifs of my intervention both with the people in the bar and with the construction workers who are indignantly and unabashedly hostile to safety. I talked to my romantic vis-a-vis about it. I was troubled that my efforts amounted to nothing, that like the opinion of other animals watching the hummingbird my efforts were futile, pointless, and even stupid. Keep in mind that my dad used to say to me, "you get no points for doing your best; I can get a baboon in here to try hard. What counts is results." (My dad knew that without his prodding I would half-ass every task given me.) But what my romantic entanglement said to me, made me think better of things. She said, "you did what was appropriate, you did enough. People like that (she was speaking of the people in the bar but might as well been talking about the construction ninnies) count on the fact that no one is watching; that no one will say something and once they recognize that someone is watching, and that people WILL confront them things will change."

I think maybe we ask too much of workers and people in general. We throw all the world's problems at them and tell them to fix them. We create lofty ideals and visions of a Utopian safety culture and leave them helpless in the face of the enormity of the problem. Maybe we had instead asked them to do just a little bit to make things safer. Maybe it's as easy as asking them to consider the example they set to new workers and colleagues who respect them, maybe we can just ask them to do what they can.

Your Mother Doesn't Work Here: Why Housekeeping Matters

(Originally published by *Fabricating & Metalworking* magazine)
The original can be found here: http://www.fabricatingandmetalworking.com/2013/09/your-mother-doesnt-work-here-why-housekeeping-matters/

Housekeeping is the manifestation of pride in your organization. A clean and well-organized workplace is the cornerstone of a robust safety management program that promotes worker safety, respect, dignity, and morale.

> The dangers of poor housekeeping are real. It saps productivity, morale and operating efficiency, yet goes largely ignored. When every competitive dollar counts, it's puzzling that more shops don't make a concerted effort to address a problem that is so easy to fix.

Perhaps the easiest — and most ignored — way to make your workplace safer is by improving your housekeeping. According to the National Safety Council (Itasca, IL), "Falls are one of the leading causes of unintentional injuries in the United States, accounting for approximately 8.9 million visits to the emergency department annually (NSC Injury Facts 2011)."

While not all slips, trips and falls are caused by housekeeping issues, a simple campaign to ensure a place for everything and that everything is in its place goes a long way toward improving not just working conditions, but safety of the workplace itself.

Housekeeping was traditionally a panicked response to a surprise visit by a customer or an audit. Workers were sent scurrying to "pick up the newspapers" as company stopped by unexpectedly. But housekeeping ought to be more than the frenzied reaction to an unplanned visit. Housekeeping is an important defense against trip hazards, accidental exposure to hazardous materials, fire hazards and a host of other nasty scenarios. Housekeeping is more than just tidying up; a robust housekeeping campaign can improve your operating efficiency in many ways beyond worker safety.

MATERIALS MANAGEMENT

Housekeeping discipline is a subset of operational discipline. A strong commitment to housekeeping can address inventory management and control (clearing stock out of the aisles and removing and disposing of scrap and obsolete equipment and stock, for example.)

SALES

When you seriously attack housekeeping, you will find that your workplace will look less like an episode of hoarders and more like a world-class operation.

I know of a manufacturer that does a fair amount of work for the U.S. government. The G-men were generally pleased with the quality, cost, and delivery of the products the shop built, but were consistently disappointed by the physical condition of the plant: the facility was cramped and crowded with trash and stock strewn around the production area; it simply didn't look very professional.

Once the company undertook a safety campaign that included a 5S program (a Japanese concept of workplace organization that places a high priority on housekeeping), the government representatives immediately took notice. The feds who came in on surprise inspections were struck by the cleanliness of the plant and actually increased their orders. While the increase in business was certainly the result of multiple factors, a clean and orderly workplace made the decision to source the work to the manufacturer easier and more defensible.

ENGAGEMENT

According to bestselling author and employee engagement expert Dr. Paul Marciano, employee engagement is about respect; workers who feel respected by their employers are far more likely to be engaged than those who feel disrespected.

Good housekeeping is a key indicator of respect; you can easily gauge the level of respect employers have for their workers — and how workers about themselves — simply by looking at their housekeeping practices. Good housekeeping isn't the result of panic-cleaning, spring cleaning, or even cleaning up once a day. Good housekeeping is the result of a clearly cast expectation of respect, i.e., the product of an expectation of respect for oneself, one's colleagues, and one's work place.

Housekeeping is the manifestation of pride in your organization. A clean and well-organized workplace is the cornerstone of a robust safety management program that promotes worker safety, respect, dignity, and morale.

MAINTENANCE
One of the biggest offenders of poor housekeeping is the maintenance department. Often, removing obsolete equipment or fixtures, cleaning dross or offal, or just plain picking up after oneself is seemingly impossible for many maintenance workers. The clutter caused by poor housekeeping practices on the part of maintenance is truly embarrassing in some organizations.

Why is it so difficult for maintenance to pick up after itself? One reason is the permitting process. Even organizations that are otherwise good at housekeeping often struggle with seeing the work orders and permits through to completion. Final project cleanup is often overlooked and — because it isn't checked — is often seen as a non-priority.

In other cases, it isn't clear to whom a housekeeping duty falls. Who is responsible for keeping tools and equipment clean, in serviceable condition, and free from damage?

EFFICIENCY
It's just plain easier to get things done in a neat and well-organized work area. In addition to preventing incidents, good housekeeping saves

space, time, and money. Work is completed with minimal waste and be done with minimal effort.

WHAT ARE THE RISKS ASSOCIATED WITH POOR HOUSEKEEPING?

For organizations that are content to work in squalor, selling the need for good housekeeping can be tough. After all, what's the risk of a little clutter? As it turns out, plenty.

Poor housekeeping can be directly linked to:

Slip, trips, and falls. According to OSHA "Slips, trips, and falls constitute the majority of general industry accidents. They cause 15 percent of all accidental deaths and are second only to motor vehicles as a cause of fatalities."

The situation is equally dire elsewhere, the Canadian Centre for Occupational Health and Safety reports that "in Canada, over 42,000 workers get injured annually due to fall accidents. This number represents about 17 percent of the "time-loss injuries" that were accepted by workers' compensation boards or commissions across Canada", and a European report in QBE Insurance Issues Forum reports that slips, trips and falls account for 37 percent of Health & Safety Executive reported accidents, and over 50 percent of public related injuries.

Increased fire hazards. Clutter, poorly labeled materials, flammable liquids left out or improperly stored, and other mess not only create a fire hazard they also can block emergency evacuation routes and impede rescue attempts.

Combustible dust. Combustible dust is a growing problem in industry and, in almost all combustible dust explosions, poor housekeeping has played an instrumental role in the disaster.

Exposure risks. Depending on your processes, poor housekeeping may lead to a higher probability of worker exposures to hazardous substances like asbestos, silica, or a host of other toxins.

Mobile Vehicle and Pedestrian Incidents. Poor housekeeping increases the need to handle materials and congests the flow of materials. Stock is misplaced, left to block pedestrian aisle ways and creates blind spots that can easily lead to serious workplace injuries.

Good housekeeping doesn't just happen, but if you expect — no, demand — good housekeeping practices for your workplace, then you are on the road to success. But demanding good housekeeping isn't enough. To achieve a sustainable housekeeping approach:

Allow workers time to clean up. This is a standard industrial engineering principle. You should budget enough time for workers to police and clean their work areas; it won't get done unless you allot time for clean-up.

Be consistent in your expectations. Cleanliness never sleeps, and you can't excuse lapses in housekeeping for any reason.

Provide supplies. Workers are far more likely to clean their work areas if they have appropriate and sufficient supplies to do so. Keep a cabinet full of cleaning supplies, brooms, mops, and fox tails that workers can use to clean their work areas.

Set an example. Only a hypocrite will expect workers to keep their work areas clean while working in an executive pig sty.

Even though the dangers of poor housekeeping are real, and it saps productivity, morale, and operating efficiency the problem goes largely ignored. In a world where every dollar counts it's puzzling that more organizations don't make a more concerted effort to address a problem that is so easy to fix.

The Rise of the Safety Jihadist

I write provocative material. I deliberately try to elicit a visceral response and take people to a place where they can explore their deepest held beliefs and question basic ideologies of safety. The latest in neuroscience suggests that our decisions are made in the part of the brain that controls emotion, and some theorize that not only are our decisions based on emotion, when we think we are looking for logical arguments for and against our decision we are really just looking for information that justifies what we want to do emotionally. Similarly, our ability to change resides deep in our subconscious beneath our defenses. When something strikes a nerve at that level it can be difficult to have a rational conversation, but in general, if one can at least reconsider one's belief set maybe it's worth a try.

Why is it important to reexamine our deepest held beliefs? Because the world is a dynamic place and if our beliefs are static we become increasingly out of touch. If we cling blindly to our beliefs and lash out to anyone who threatens our worldview then we run the risk of becoming completely and dangerously out of touch with the realities of your profession and become a useless relic. That should be career suicide, but sadly even the most out of touch hacks can usually find work based on their years and years of experience. But what good is 40.2 years of experience if that experience consists chiefly of self-congratulatory affirmations and retreads of theories that are a century old.

Not that every new idea is a good one. There is as much crap spewed by the idea du jour pundits today as there ever has been. And just because an idea or theory is new doesn't make it any better than conventional wisdom, but it's important that any professional consider new ideas and emerging thought with an open mind.

That's getting tougher and tougher to do in safety, owing to the rise in extremist thought in safety. The merest suggestion that we discard a safety truism is likely to create nothing short of a public outrage. Take for instance the response to Heinrich's Pyramid. A recent thread on the social networking site LinkedIn elicited 3,186 comments ranging from the intellectually bantering to the crackpot personal attacks. The thread quoted a recent assertion by EHS Today:

"Heinrich's assertion that 88% of accidents are the result of unsafe acts has been dismissed as something he just made up. There was no research behind it whatsoever. "and asked the simple question "What's your opinion? And why?"

According to a recent article by Ashley Johnson in H+S Magazine, a poll the magazine conducted found that 86% of respondents believed either completely or somewhat in Heinrich's theories, while another 10% reporting that they weren't familiar with Heinrich's theories. The article is a scathing indictment of Heinrich's theories from experts who question his methods, his conclusions, and generally speaking nearly everything he had to say. The article was balanced by a half-hearted defense that the numbers were never meant to be statistical predictors (they were, by the way) and that Heinrich never blamed the workers (he did. In fact, Heinrich was a devotee of eugenics and believed that one's race and ethnicity played a factor in the likelihood that a worker would be injured or cause an injury to other.)

What does this all have to do with extremism? Plenty. This demonstrates that despite a growing body of evidence to the contrary a deeply held belief will hold sway. This in itself is not extremism, but it does create an environment where extremists thrive. Why do people cling to beliefs that are refuted (there are still people who deeply believe in fake photos and film footage of the Loch Ness Monster and Bigfoot, even though the perpetrators of these hoaxes[1])? People tend to want to believe in what they're doing and react with fear and anger (even aggression) when people chip away at the foundation.

It's not just the Heinrich supporters who will lash out against any suggestion that doesn't support their worldview. If you don't believe me just publish something critical about Behavior Based Safety. Within hours extremists and fanatics will marshal their forces and begin attacking you. The problem has grown to such an extent that several editors of leading safety magazines actively avoid the debate more out of a desire to avoid arguing with fanatics than out of fear or intimidation. But intimidation of the press is a goal of extremists everywhere —from Al Qaida to the Ku Klux Klan to the Neo-Nazis to the safety extremists—is to discredit, attack, intimidate, and generally silence the media which, if it is truly unbiased—will never buy their bill of goods.

Extremism Is Rooted in Fear

Let's suppose you have 40.2 years of experience in safety where you served with distinction, and someone comes along and asserts something contrary to the foundation on which your entire experience is predicated. It's the equivalent of having a Ph.D. in economics from an East Berlin University. What happens to your credentials and accomplishments and your very identity as a safety professional when all on which it is built crumbles? People will protect their beliefs with a wildness typically reserved for mother grizzlies defending their cubs; they will make ugly personal attacks and seek to gather together like-minded souls close to them.

Extremism Loves Company

Social networking sites make it easy to reach out to a world of people. Some credit social networking with ushering in Arab Spring, but it also has a darker side. Social Networking affords us the opportunity for the fanatics to get their ideas out to a sympathetic ear. Unfortunately, when it comes to safety, people are dying in the workplace while crackpots are postulating theories that are given equal weight with responsible theorists in safety. I will leave the readers to decide which slide of the equation on which I fall.

[1] I'm speaking of the most famous Loch Ness monster photo and the actual film footage of a reputed Bigfoot. The very people who first produced them convincingly have admitted that they perpetrated a fraud and disproved both of these, "best pieces of evidence". If you want to believe in the Loch Ness monster or Bigfoot God bless you, but what was the most compelling evidence has been disproven. And don't even get me started on crop circles.

CHAPTER 3

Deming on Safety

One of the greatest minds on process improvements has largely ignored in Worker Safety. Edward Deming's 14 points can easily be adapted into a roadmap for a robust and highly effective safety management system. Unfortunately, many in the safety community refuse to try to learn from Deming's writings for reasons known only to them.

The 14 Points of Workplace Safety
Deming On Safety

(Originally published in Fabricating & Metalworking it can be found here: https://workersafetynet.wordpress.com/2011/07/17/deming-on-safety-part-1-constancy-of-purpose-for-safety/) Reprinted with permission.

By merging the engineering discipline, process control and business acumen of W. Edwards Deming to the practical world of employee protection, Phil La Duke of Rockford Greene International introduces some profound principles of worker safety that are an absolute must for manufacturers.

1. SAFETY IS NOT YOUR NUMBER ONE PRIORITY

If safety were truly your number one priority you would close your doors and mothball your business. Your number one priority should always be the continued survival of your business. Anyone who tells you different is either a liar or a fool.

That having been said, you won't be in business long if you don't effectively manage safety. Safety is neither a priority nor a goal; instead it is a criterion by which manufacturers measure the efficacy of its efforts to be successful. Safety is a strategic business element that needs to be managed as scrupulously as quality, delivery, cost and morale.

2. MISTAKES ARE INEVITABLE, INJURIES ARE NOT

People make mistakes; it's practically embedded in our DNA. Stop trying to remind people not to make mistakes and focus instead on preventing the injuries that so predictably happen when people screw up. You may not prevent every injury, but that doesn't make it impossible.

FMEAs and other predictive tools should be used to identify areas of greatest risk and efforts should be made to reduce the risk of injuries to the lowest praticible level. The true benefit in this point is the belief that it is possible and the disappointment we feel anytime we aren't successful in prevention.

3. FOCUS ON PREVENTION

Preventing injuries is more efficient than reacting to them. If you spend your money preventing injuries you will spend less money overall. Stop thinking that you might get lucky and avoid a serious and costly injury; you won't. Injuries are typically caused by failures in the system. By managing hazards (procedural, behavioral, and mechanical) organizations can reduce unplanned downtime, injuries, and defects.

4. MOVE BEYOND COMPLIANCE

Compliance with the government regulations is important and tends to correlate to a process that is in control. But we can never mistake being compliant with being safe. Stop congratulating yourself for doing only that which is mandated by the government; you get no credit for doing what you were always supposed to have been doing.

5. INSTILL UNIVERSAL OWNERSHIP AND ACCOUNTABILITY FOR SAFETY

Every job plays a role in ensuring workplace safety. Everyone must be answerable when processes and protocols fail to keep workers safe. Hold workers accountable for eliminating hazards rather than for injuries.

6. SHIFT THE OWNERSHIP OF SAFETY TO OPERATIONS

Operations has the greatest control and oversight of the safety of the workplace. Operations leadership should conduct routine reviews of key safety metrics. Safety as a function should be instructive and should help Operations to be more efficient.

7. THE ABSENCE OF INJURIES DOES NOT NECESSARILY DENOTE THE PRESENCE OF SAFETY

Safety is an expression of probability. No situation is ever 100 percent risk free. Safety must be managed in terms of risk not by taking a body count.

8. AVOID SHAME AND BLAME POLICIES AND TACTICS

Workers do not want to get hurt and manufacturing processes are not supposed to hurt them; no amount of behavior modification will change this.

9. INVEST IN BASIC SKILLS TRAINING

The best way to ensure worker safety is by providing them with good foundational training in the tasks they are routinely expected to do. People who are skilled at the basic tasks associated with their jobs are far less likely to be injured.

10. END SAFETY GIMMICKS

There is a cottage industry devoted to taking your money in the name of safety rewards. Incentives should only be used to reward active participation in safety, not to reward an absence of reported injuries. Frankly, why isn't coming home in one-piece reward enough?

Most workers I've talked to find safety incentives condescending and somewhat insulting. As one put it, "They give us a pizza party at the end of the month if we don't kill anyone. It's as if they think the only reason we will ever work safe is for the pizza".

11. STOP COMPARING YOUR SAFETY PERFORMANCE TO THE INDUSTRY AVERAGE

Measuring an organization's safety record relative to the broader industry average is meaningless and should be abandoned. Instead, use a combination of lagging and leading indicators to attain a more meaningful view of your overall performance in safety.

12. ENCOURAGE BETTER DECISION MAKING

People take risks and that is not necessarily a bad thing. Our policies and procedures can never cover every contingency. We need to invest in training to help our workers to avoid making bad judgment calls and stupid decisions.

13. STOP LETTING SAFETY BLAME OPERATIONS FOR ITS OWN INADEQUACIES

Whenever I suggest a substantive change in how the Safety function does business, I am invariably told that the Operations leadership will never support my idea. Safety must be a key resource to Operations and stop whining every time it doesn't get its way.

Instead of impeding Operations and hampering its progress, Safety must support Operations to find safe ways of accomplishing organizational goals instead of working at cross-purposes with Production. Safety needs to get out of the business of telling Operations "no" and Operations must collaborate with Safety to reduce risk as much as is practical.

14. STOP TRYING TO MANIPULATE WORKERS' BEHAVIORS

Safety is not about managing people's behavior; it's about managing risk. Behavioral psychology is overused and frequently misused in commercial safety solutions. Behavior-based safety appeals to operations executives who are looking for a magic bullet. In reality, it is too often snake oil being sold by the greedy to the dim-witted.

It's high time that we stop treating safety like it's some mystical secret. Let's stop hiding behind the platitudes and get to work. If the Safety function can't support business than it's time to get rid of it. Those safety professionals who understand the core business of the organizations in which they work should be celebrated, while those who simply collect a paycheck should be excused out the door.

Deming On Safety Point 1: Constancy of Purpose for Safety

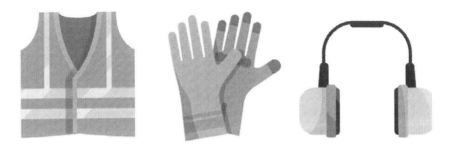

Almost a year ago, I wrote a piece on the relationship between Deming's 14 points and safety. I've been asked by many people to expand on my thoughts on this connection because the limited space afforded me in an issue of Facility Safety Management magazine (typically 1000 words) constrains me to a fairly broad examination of any topic.

In management framework that W. Edwards Deming created that eventually came to be called Deming's 14 points, Deming advocated what he called a "constancy of purpose". In his first point, Deming criticized senior business leaders for their tendency to focus on knee-jerk reactions to immediate issues and short-term solutions instead of favor of proactive long-term planning.

Certainly, constancy of purpose—the belief in the value of a long-term commitment to continual improvement— applies to safety. Deming believed that in order to create a constancy of purpose organizations require 1) innovation, 2) research and education 3) continuous improvement of product and service and 4) investment in the maintenance of equipment, furniture, fixtures, and production aids.

Innovation

I spent nine years designing, developing, and implementing one of the greatest and most important safety innovations in the history of the industry. I was able to provide each of my 18 clients a return on their investment in the first year. Most of these companies reduced their injuries by over 60% and the average reduction in workers' compensation claims were over $2.5 million annually. But the business failed. Not because it was a bad idea, but because safety professionals as a profession are a) unparalleled in their aversion to risk (and thereby innovation) and b) the deal sounded too good to be true. (Of course, one could argue that I am a crappy businessman and salesman,) So inventing better mousetrap did not end with the world beating a path to my door. Instead, it led me to join Rockford Greene, where I can turn down clients that I don't think are worth the effort to try to convince them to do something different.

But if safety is going to improve, safety professionals must embrace true safety innovations instead of chasing the empty promises of the snake oil salesmen so prevalent in safety today. Einstein said that we can't solve problems using the same thinking that we had when we created them, but then Einstein didn't work in safety.

Research and Education

I have written and spoken more than anyone should ever have to endure on the subject of the immediate link and perfect correlation between effective training and worker safety. But the point is so important that I repeat it here. People who are effectively trained and competent in their jobs are infinitely less likely to be injured on the job. But of course, scarce few people are effectively trained. Organizations must research more efficient ways to produce their goods and deliver their services and in so doing make their workplaces safer. But research alone isn't enough. There are no shortages of improvements to our processes, especially as we stabilize them. But too often these improvements fail to make it to the standard work instructions (if they exist) and instances where the organization trains the workers in the improvements are rarer still.

Continuous Improvement

A relentless desire to improve the process is key to safety. As long as there is ANY risk of worker injuries there is an opportunity for improvement and there is ALWAYS some risk of worker injury. Additionally, according to lean principles worker injuries are waste and since a primary goal of any continuous improvement effort is the elimination of all waste. Effective continuous improvement will most likely result in significant safety improvements as well as large payoffs in quality and efficiency.

Investment in Maintenance

Much to the chagrin of the snake oil salesmen who believe that nearly all injuries are caused by the clumsy, the thick-witted, or belligerent employees who ignore safety protocols the fact is, equipment wears out and when it does the result is frequently an injury.

An investment in capable, predictable equipment that supports a stable, repeatable process is the cornerstone—not only of safety—but of every quality system from Statistical Process Control to six sigma.

Creating a constancy of purpose isn't easy, but all of Deming's points are based on it. Applying this point to safety supports the range of safety activities. The constancy of purpose creates safety inspections that look beyond the checklist mentality for process improvements to reduce workplace risk; the development and deployment of safety strategies; and continuous improvement workshops focused on safety improvements.

More Deming On Safety:
Adopt the New Philosophy

Deming's second point is "Adopt the new philosophy. We are in a new economic age. Western management must awaken to the challenge, must learn their responsibilities, and take on leadership for change." In writing this point Deming could well be describing safety. For years Japanese companies have viewed the worker as a resource, as the best source of ideas for improvement, but also long-term partners in business; certainly, a wise organization would do everything in its power to preserve and nurture something so vital to its success.

Adopting the new philosophy in safety manifests itself in several important ways.

Injuries are waste and need to be managed as such. Far too many safety pundits are still preaching that "safety is the right thing to do", they continue to preach about moral imperatives for companies to protect worker at all costs. Whether or not companies have any compunction to protect workers is between them and the workers. That having been said, organizations need to protect their competitiveness, their profits, and their efficiency and all this begins with a relentless pursuit of waste reductions.

Stop worrying about changing the culture and start worrying about changing your processes. Too often safety professionals stick with what they know and don't venture too far beyond it. Unfortunately, safety professionals typically don't know all that much about organizational development, transformational change, or organizational psychology. Even so, that doesn't seem to be sufficient to stop safety vendors from shilling half-baked culture change solutions to organizations. Nor does it stop internal safety professionals from championing initiatives of which their sole qualifications are limited to reading an article in the odd safety magazine or attending a session at a safety conference.

That some organizational cultures inappropriately undervalue safety is indisputable, but making the leap that the Safety function is capable of changing that on some grand, enterprise-wide scale is laughable. On the other hand, few safety professionals understand process mapping, value stream analysis, and the other tools and methods necessary for process improvement.

Integrate the Safety into Other Business Functions. The days where Safety is a separate business function are rapidly coming to a close. Maintaining a safety infrastructure with Safety professionals must end. Just as the Quality function evolved into a vehicle for process improvement so too must safety. As long as Safety professionals see themselves as discrete from the overall operations and somehow able to operate in isolation from production it will always be at risk of being dropped from the corporate team.

Leadership Must Advocate for Change. Leaders are often maligned by safety professionals. Too many times safety professionals blame their own failures on a lack of leadership commitment. In this case, Safety professionals are right: Leaders SHOULD be visible and outspoken advocates for safety and organizational change that supports it. That's not to say that safety professionals shouldn't play a role in this initiative. Safety professionals should provide expertise and guidance to leaders, many of whom, don't know how to begin to advocate change.

If safety professionals are going to be trusted counselors to the leaders, there is much work they need to do:

Quit pretending to know more than they do. Safety is an area of expertise that requires practitioners to have a deep understanding of a diverse range of disciplines, but there are limits to even the most learned safety professionals' curricula verities. There is a natural tendency (bordering on compulsion) for safety professionals to advise far beyond their knowledge base and once labeled a vacuous windbag it's hard to be seen as having any opinion of value to offer.

Research and Analysis. Perhaps the most useful service a safety professional can offer is comprehensive research coupled with razor-sharp analysis on the best way to leverage the things uncovered by the research.

Offer Guidance, Not Advice or Opinions. One of the most important thing that I recently learned is that offering guidance is tough. Frequently, what we see as guidance is opinion or just plain butting in. Guidance is marked more by listening than by advising someone as to what they had ought to do. Guidance is invited; advice or opinions are not. Safety professionals need to transition to trusted counselors than pouting eunuchs that huff and sigh when they don't get their ways. But offering guidance requires trust, and trust takes time to build.

Recognize the Realities and Challenges Endemic to the New Global Economy. Deming developed his 14 points over 50 years ago, yet even then he was able to recognize that even then we were in a new economic reality. Even as safety comes under increasing government scrutiny the scarcity of resources available for workplace safety continues to plague safety professionals. The stark reality is that while the number of demands placed on safety increase, the resources are shrinking or trending flat.

Improve the quality of safety training and ensure its efficacy. My background is in organizational development and training and I will say unequivocally that the most safety training is wholly inadequate for anything except for checking the compliance box. The biggest opportunity to transform the safety of the workplace lies in the improvements that can be made in training. The better a worker is prepared for the tasks associated with his or her job the safer that worker will be. I wrote an article on how safety training could be improved,

What's Wrong with Safety Training and How to Fix It so I won't revisit it here.

Deming's work remains the quintessential guide to quality, but the lessons one can glean and apply to safety are timeless and substantial. In studying Deming's thoughts on quality we can transform safety and in so doing our industries.

Deming Point 3

Reputation

As you read this book, you are likely to have already noticed some repetition. And while this repetition is not deliberate it is unavoidable. What you are reading was not written at the same time or as one long piece, rather it is the product of blog posts and magazine articles spanning more than a decade. One could rightfully ask why I didn't more carefully craft the book into a more seamless and less repetitive work (one could also write their own damn book and do as they please.) I deliberately kept the repetition in, because repetition fosters learning. Maybe if the stubbornly ignorant and blissfully stupid hear something enough time it will make an impact. So with that having been said, let us move on to Deming's 3 Point and apply it to safety.

"Cease dependence on inspection to achieve quality. Eliminate the need for massive inspection by building quality into the product in the first place."

The equivalent of the circa 1970 quality inspector is the safety observation, an asinine practice where one employee or supervisor watches another worker do his or her job and then critiques them. This activity is central to all Behavior Based Safety programs and it is also its principle flaw.

Reason 1: The Observations are Pointless

First of all, the safety observation ignores the Hawthorne Effect. This phenomenon was discovered in 1958 when a researcher analyzed data gathered from a study from 1924-1932 a the Hawthorne Works in Cicero, Illinois. Researchers at the time experimented with the effects of lighting on worker productivity. The results they found surprised them and they concluded that just being observed and the object of increased attention increased worker productivity and performance. It didn't matter what they did to the lights±—brighten them and the workers improved. Dim them and the workers improved. The changes in behavior weren't because of the lighting it was because the workers were being observed. Subsequent research has shown that research subjects act differently when they are observed, EVEN IF THEY DON'T KNOW THEY ARE BEING OBSERVED. So it seems fairly idiotic to expect to gain any meaningful insights from standing around watching someone work, knowing that said work is likely significantly different from the norm.

Reason 2: The Observations are condescending

How arrogant is it to watch another person doing a job and point out the things that they could be doing safer? This is a person who has been doing a job far longer than I have (if they have done it at all) presumes to tell ME how to do it better. Several years ago I was the Safety Production Consultant on Transformers V: The Last Night, and action picture filmed in some pretty hairy locations, not the least of which was the Packard Plant, the oldest abandoned factory in North America if not the world. It is a highly sought movie set because it looks downright unearthly. Those of you who have never worked on a movie set might be surprised at how simultaneously overwhelming and mundane it can be. It's overwhelming because a production site can be the size of a small city and teeming with people who work in trades both familiar and strange. The faces are all unfamiliar to you and you don't know who can fire you. It's mundane because much of the work is building sets, tearing down sets, painting, carpentry, electrical work, working from heights—in other words, things the average safety guy sees every day. Personally, I found the cast and crew—who know full well that even a relatively minor injury can end their careers—cared a great deal about safety, but I also found they also knew how to do their jobs very well.

When I got on set (I was responsible for something like 36 different sites) I would first introduce myself, by saying, "Hi, I'm Phil La Duke, and I a different kind of safety guy. I'm here to watch your back not to be on your back. I'm not here to police you or to tell you how to do your job. I am here to help you make informed decisions about the risks you take. I would then say, "forgive me, but what do you do?" They would answer by giving me their job titles, and I would clarify things. "No, I mean what do you DO?" They would walk me through the tasks that they would be doing that day after which I would say, "What could go wrong that could cause you to get injured; what should I be looking for?" They would walk through the various things that were the highest risks and we would talk about how we could mitigate the risks. THEY told ME. After a while, I would just walk up and say, "hey guys what are we working on today?" and "What safety concerns do you have?" I got to really like those guys and I'd to think they liked me. They would routinely point out their concerns and I would make sure they got addressed by the appropriate people. They saw me as a resource to help them protect themselves by doing the legwork that they didn't have time to do. That is FAR different from me being some condescending asshat that smugly watches them struggle and then tells them they're doing it wrong.

Reason 3: Observations can cause conflict.

Recently one of my blog readers wrote to me and asked me yet again to write my opinion of Behavior-Based Safety in a blog. Reluctantly I did, and predictably people who continue to shovel this horse-shit for a living attacked me; I also pissed of chiropractors but what are they gonna do adjust my spine? (Hunter Thompson may not have had any qualms about pissing of outlaw bikers, but I stick to pissing of members professions against which I figure I can pretty well hold my own. The reason he wanted me to address it was his company was adopting a BBS system and he had reservations. "They don't teach you how to respond to a worker you've observed telling you to @#$% off." For the record, that is EXACTLY how I would have reacted when I was 25 and working an assembly line, right before I called for my Union committeeman and filed a grievance for double supervision (most contracts hold that only your direct supervisor can criticize you and the feedback that was given in an Observation could be argued as violating this contractual obligation. Even in a non-Union shop Observations often pit worker against worker and this increases the risk of injury not decreases it.

Reason 4: It creates a costly bureaucracy.

I can assure you, paying one worker a wage to produce nothing more than an observation card is costly. I can also assure you that if you are costing the company money you had better make damned sure you can demonstrate a return on that investment. If you don't when the ax swings you will (and should) have a giant bullseye on your neck. Companies can't exist if they continually spend money that adds as much value as throwing it down a sewer drain.

There's a better way.

Frontline supervision is ultimately responsible for workplace safety (you can be working safely and some other idiot can kill you because he or she was not. Frontline supervisors have the control of the work area and have the authority to intercede to correct unsafe behaviors and physical conditions. Of course, you should look out for your own safety, but looking out for hazards around you can be difficult if you are focused on your job. I can hear frustrated supervisors screaming that they can't be everywhere, but they CAN have a one-on-one conversation at the job-site and ask if the worker has any safety concerns. If a supervisor is too busy to do that then he or she has no business being a supervisor. These conversations build trust and respect which are critical components of worker empowerment, and worker empowerment is one of the single greatest determinants of success in safety and everything else in the workplace.

Point 4: Instill Universal Ownership and Accountability for Safety

Safety ACCOUNTABILITY

My 14 points for safety was one-part homage to W. Edward Deming and two parts an attempt to identify in broad strokes the cumulation of my experience, education, and internalization of my body of work around worker safety, a journey of learning I undertook some 40 years ago and one, God willing, I will continue for some time. Every so often I explore these points in a bit more depth. In this subchapter, I explore my fourth point.

My fourth point for worker safety is:

"Instill Universal Ownership and Accountability for Safety: Every Job plays a role in ensuring workplace safety and everyone must be accountable when procedures fail to keep workers safe."

I have always been leery of slogans like "Safety is everybody's job" chiefly because I've come to learn that when something becomes everyone's job it effectively becomes nobody's job.

When it comes to lowering workplace risk of injury (or workplace productivity for that matter) everyone plays a role, and everyone must know one's role, own one's role, and be accountable for the successful completion of the duties of one's role.

The safety of the workplace is a complex system with many interdependencies; a vast network of links and connections and like a chain a safety system is only as good as its weakest link.

Everyone who interacts with this system has certain duties:

1. Duty to comply with a standard. Each person (be he or she the CEO or a visitor) needs to under and comply with the safety procedures appropriate to one's position and activity. Additionally, one has a duty to perform one's job as designed. Working out of station increases the risk to the worker but adds variation and risk to anyone who interacts with the system.

2. Duty to actively reduce risk. People tend to think about safety in individual terms when in fact when they take unjustifiable risks it can cause an injury or system failure anywhere in the system.

3. Duty to reduce variation and risk in the work and work environment. All workers must be the acknowledged owner of safety. They must be expected and allowed to police and enforce the safety of their jobs and spheres of influences. Their authority over the safety of the work area must be acknowledged, supported, and respected.

4. Duty to Know One's Duties. A lack of training or awareness of safety expectations can never be allowed to excuse one's failure to behave in an unsafe manner or to knowingly fail to contain a hazard. If one has not been informed of all hazards one has the responsibility to seek out this information.

Deming On Safety Point 5: Improve the System

"Improve constantly and forever the system of production and service, to improve quality and productivity, and thus constantly decrease costs."—W. Edward Deming's Fourth Point

This is the fifth work I have done that explores the relationship between Deming's 14 points and safety. Deming's fourth point, "Improve constantly and forever the system of production and service, to improve quality and productivity, and thus constantly decrease costs" applies fairly directly to safety.

Safety professionals often lose sight of their responsibility for increasing efficiency and increasing profitability, preferring instead to see their job as a noble calling removed from the vulgarities of making money. At the same time that safety professionals bemoan their lack of credibility in the eyes of Operations leadership, many safety professionals either stand idly disconnected from operations or actively promoting junk science and the latest in safety fads.

The safety function not only can contribute to cost reductions and process improvement, it can lead it. Worker injuries are expensive and wasteful. No one derives any benefit from a workplace injury and beyond the cost of treating the injury the costs are considerable and can make the cost of doing business significantly higher. From increased insurance rates to the negative publicity the costs associated with a single injury can have tentacles that touch many areas.

There are several areas in which safety professionals can reduce costs and increase efficiency, both within the safety function and without. Safety professionals should begin measuring the cost of operating its own function. Establishing a baseline serves several purposes. First, a baseline makes it easy to see, in real costs how much safety costs the operation. Once the safety professional has identified the expenses associated with running the department he or she should express the costs in a way that is meaningful to the organization. For some organizations, the cost should be expressed as a percentage of sales, while for others it can be described in terms of the product or service the company sells. But whatever the trigger, describing the cost in terms that matter is paramount to a safety professional's success. From there, the safety professional should chart and display the cost in an area of the organization where management decisions are made.

Advertising how much the safety function costs to maintain may seem foolhardy to some, but this kind of data sharing shows the organization that the safety function understands how business works and sees itself as accountable for delivering at least as much value as any other function. Of course, once the safety function has announced the amount it costs the organization the safety professionals need to quickly take action to reduce those costs, and the fastest way to reduce costs is to eliminate waste.

There is waste in any process, and what's more, there are even more non-value-added activities. Waste is anything that costs money but returns nothing worthwhile. Safety professionals need to identify the things that are unnecessary, overly costly, or where the cost is disproportionate to the savings. It can be tough to quantify the return on investment for safety, but it is easy to take a look at discretionary purchases and dial back the ones that you know intuitively aren't worth it.

Sawing the pencils in half will only take you so far, and eventually the safety professional will have to improve the processes that safety uses to support operations. Process inefficiencies are a major contributor to costs, and the safety function is far from immune from these costs. Fortunately, most companies have process improvement processes and teams that can help the safety function to fine-tune the way it does business and reduce the cost of doing business.

Outside of the safety function, safety professionals need to quantify the costs of the organization's safety record and demonstrate improvements over time that directly correlate to the initiatives planned and executed by the safety department. Things like the safety BINGO, children's safety poster contests, and similarly flakey feel-good programs that cost more than they can ever hope to return don't qualify for consideration and should be scrapped. Safety professionals need to be careful not to be overly protective of their pet projects or to claim responsibility for improvements that they can't cleanly prove. Deming would perhaps take things even further and recommend that safety avoid any undertaking that cannot be directly linked to process, improvement productivity improvements and cost reductions.

Just as with the cost reductions within the safety function, safety professionals should track and display the savings of reduced injuries. Communicating the contributions that the safety function makes to the company's bottom line or the organization's efficiency increases is an important way to link the goals of the safety function with the overall goals of the organization. As Deming observed, continuous improvement is everyone's job.

The idea that safety should shift its focus away from saving lives in favor of saving money may seem distasteful to some, even insulting perhaps. But as long as safety professions view themselves as philosophical loggerheads, safety professionals will never be seen as equal partners in the organization's success. If the goal of safety is to save lives while the goal of the organization remains to make money, the two set themselves at odds and as Abraham Lincoln once said, "a house divided against itself cannot stand."

Deming On Safety Pt. 6: Point 6 Institute Training On the Job

In the interest of full disclosure, I should tell you that I am a training nerd, a lean nerd, a manufacturing nerd and a performance improvement nerd. I hold a certificate in Training, Design and Development from the University of Michigan and have worked for many years helping companies to improve. When I was ultimately hired to help UAW-DaimlerChrysler to develop the Bringing Excellence to Safety Teams (B.E.S.T.) initiative I was able to connect and bring to bear all I knew about Lean and Performance Improvement to the world of Worker Safety.

Years later, as I designed and built SafetyIMPACT! for my employer I took pains to consider how Deming would view all the innovations we were making to safety. For the record, this isn't a commercial. I'm not trying to get any of you to hire me (although it wouldn't kill you to hire me to consult, would it?) But I have found it astonishing how few safety professionals are able to understand that Deming's principles not only apply to quality, but they make the job of the safety professional easier.

Nowhere is the connection between Deming's 14 points and worker safety better illustrated than in point 6: Institute training on the job. It sounds pretty rudimentary, doesn't it? Is there anyone working in any industry today that doesn't intuitively understand the link between the quality of the product and the efficacy of the training the worker receives? In fairness to Deming, effective training has not always been the norm. In 1985 I was hired as a hardware installer in the cushion room of the General Motors Fleetwood Plant. The building was built circa 1890 and originally produced coaches for horse-and-buggy carriages. It was a six-story hulking brute that sat hunched at the base of the Rouge River Bridge. My job was to install seat locks (the—often jagged— pieces of metal about a foot long that held the seat bottom to the back.) The job was literally backbreaking work at a time when OSHA was a neophyte and little was done to protect workers. My training consisted of shadowing Randy, a good-natured, burly, seldom sober, experienced worker. Randy had just won his bid on a plumb assignment (assembling armrests) that he could do in 5 hours while drunk or high on cocaine. To be fair, Randy taught me well. In those days safety glasses weren't required so if I wasn't careful tiny metal slivers would blow into my eyes. Randy also recommended that I get a pair of steel toed shoes even though they too weren't required. Not everything that Randy taught me was sterling. I learned that my unusually long air hose (procured using charm and back channel connections so I could work out of my workstation, or "up the line" and get a couple more seconds of butt time) was a trip hazard by doing just that and cracking my wrist on a metal frame of conveyor belt. I learned that installing a recliner frame incorrectly would spiral the seat or the 15lb metal part at my head. And most painfully, I learned that the sharp metal parts would easily destroy my cloth gloves and I needed to steal a fresh pair for after lunch. A second pair was deemed too costly and forbidden.

So Deming's advice wasn't so condescending after all. But maybe there is more (something obvious) to Deming's fifth point. Safety training and the odorous Behaviour Based Safety has become more than a cottage industry; its big business. And Government regulations mean that many organizations (fearful that customized training might not meet the requirements) exclusively use training designed for the widest possible audience. I don't think Deming would be happy with safety training that is conducted in a classroom without any context. I prefer to interpret this particular point literally, that is, I think Deming would recommend that safety training, to the extent possible, be conducted at the workstation under the exact working conditions. This means that if there are hazards associated with a particular chemical used in a given job, the worker should be trained in how to read the Material Safety Data

Sheet for that chemical as he is using the chemical for the first time.

Just the term, "Safety Training" would probably give Deming the willies. Is there any training in production that isn't related to safety? Even an office job has ergonomic considerations that should be addressed in word processing or spreadsheet software training. In fact, there are scarce few instances where safety shouldn't be a primary concern in training of any sort. Years ago, I was a consultant to Ford where I helped it develop a hybrid focus factory approach in the U.S. and Hungary. I began every training course. I developed with an exploration of the safety in the context of performing the specific tasks being performed. Sure, we had training that we purchased, but it was to augment (and truthfully to ensure compliance) training that we custom-designed for the operation. I believe now as I believed then that the most powerful and effective safety training is that which is seamlessly embedded into the job aids, Standard Work Instructions, and training courses used to teach workers how to successfully do their jobs.

My personal experience with safety goes even further back, however. Prior to my job at General Motors I worked as a security guard at a Nuclear Power Plant. While I can't tell you much about my experiences there for obvious reasons, I can say unequivocally that every bit of training I received not only had safety embedded in it but also had safety overtones. Some of you might be surprised just how dangerous some ordinarily innocuous conditions can be in a nuclear context. Learning to do my job and learning to do my job safely were the same thing.

There is a growing movement in worker safety to create a "safety culture" and unfortunately most of the people selling these services know less than squat about organizational change or culture. You already have a safety culture, in that your company has some view of safety. Safety is a value within your organizations. Some organizations place a great deal of value on safety and other do not. I guess I am just arguing semantics here so please forgive me. If you want your culture to place a higher value and importance on safety start by improving your training. Training is where respect and demand for safety are fostered, reinforced, and where the demand for it is created.

Deming On Safety: Point 7

"Institute leadership. The aim of supervision should be to help people and machines and gadgets to do a better job. Supervision of management is in need of an overhaul, as well as supervision of production workers." —W. Edward Deming's 7th Point.

Deming saw quality as bigger than a single function and I think this is equally true of safety. In point seven, Deming enjoins organizations to "overhaul the supervision of management as well as the supervision of production workers." I would add, "the function and supervision of safety should also be overhauled." I've made it no secret that I think that the Safety function should be overhauled. What Deming saw as a fatal flaw in business was that managers saw their jobs as being primarily associated with making sure workers didn't lollygag, steal, and screw things up. If the aim of supervision is to help people and machines and gadgets do a better job, by necessity the role of supervision is to help workers to do their jobs more safely.

People talk a lot about the need to do a better job in implementing a culture that values safety, but this is misguided. Safety should be a non-negotiable criterion that embeds everything we do. Just as the "Quality is Job #1" signs were torn down so to should the signs reminding people not to die on the job. The terms "safety" and "quality" are often used as if they are finite, quantifiable terms when in reality they are qualitative terms. If you are like me, you probably struggle with the difference between qualitative and quantitative measures (hey, we shouldn't feel that bad about our confusion, the words look and sound a lot alike and describe really similar things.) Quantitative measures are usually counted measures. These measures talk about whether something is present or not or describes how many widgets we have in stock. You get quantitative measures by counting things. Qualitative measurements describe the quality of something and that means there is often no absolute standard. We use ± to describe qualitative measures. Qualitative measures, in other words, are relative; like safety (or quality). At what point can we ever pronounce something completely safe? When we describe something as "safe" we are usually saying that it is "safer" than something else. Because "safety" is a relative term, supervisors should be looking for ways to help make people and machines and gadgets do a safer job. To do this the organization needs to invest in leadership. People often mistake "supervision" or "management" for leadership and this causes problems. A supervisor watches a population to ensure compliance, a manager stewards resources to ensure they are used most expeditiously, but a leader engages people so that they know what the right thing to do is and they do it because they know that doing the right thing is what is expected of them.

I have often heard safety professionals complain about a lack of support from "leadership". I know I am arguing semantics when I say this, but safety professionals ARE leaders or at least they are supposed to be. I understand that when I hear safety professionals whining that leadership doesn't support them they are talking about people above their pay grades, but I find the choice of the word "leader" as particularly illuminating and damning. The first step in overhauling the safety function is to take a hard look at the lack of leadership at the highest ranks of safety in organizations.

Human resources and talent development functions should be aggressively building Operations leadership that understands safety and the need to hardwire safety into every aspect of what we do. Not because it's the right thing to do, but because injuries are so destructive to our core business. Let me illustrate: Last night I was having a beer with a couple of guys who were telling me about their business, a small fabrication shop. The topic turned to safety because the shop had just had a recordable injury after a saw blade broke and cut one of their best finishers. He went to the hospital and received stitches in his head and was out for a day and a half. What did this injury cost the company? The medical treatment, the rise in the company's insurance rate, overtime to replace the worker's capacity for a shift and a half, the loss of production meant that they couldn't ship the part via normal shipping and the salesman had to drive the part over 1,000 miles round-trip (he got a speeding ticket, but we won't count that cost). And the insurance rates went up about $40,000 a year. I'm sorry to disappoint you but the company didn't have enough money to pay for a full-time safety professional, so I don't have an accurate figure of the hard costs, nor can I give you a figure for the loss of productivity associated with the other people gawking around, loss of reputation, and a host of other hidden costs. The company learned a costly lesson about the cost of injuries. A safety leader, a true professional whose credibility is such that people listen to him or her could have fostered an environment where regular productive maintenance was performed on the saw that would likely have a) identified that a safety device had been removed b) taught the operator how to inspect the equipment before using it c) predicted approximately when the blade would fail, and d) communicate this knowledge to maintenance and the operator.

Would these actions have prevented the accident? Maybe not, but this approach would have greatly reduced the probability of failure. In a very real sense, if Deming's view of leadership comes to fruition, we won't need a tactical safety guy. The supervisors and area managers become the new safety guy. The safety professional should move into a more consultative role. The safety professional should inform business strategy—not safety strategy—such that the production leaders can tap into the safety professional's knowledge of regulations, best practices, and other specialized expertise.

Deming On Safety: Part 8

> "Drive out fear, so that everyone may work effectively for the company."—W. Edward Deming's 8th Point.

Of all of W. Edward Deming's points, none resonates quite so deeply with me than his eighth point, "Drive out fear, so that everyone may work effectively for the company." While each of his points is directly relatable to the field and function of safety, perhaps this point is more than merely relatable, it is the foundation of safety.

Sure, safety means not getting injured, and yes, safety means that one is operating at a relatively low probability of injury, but at its core, safety means freedom from fear. As anyone who was around an organization when it tried to implement process improvement in the world of quality can attest, driving fear out of an organization isn't easy, in fact, it's damned difficult.

If we have any hope of creating a culture that values and encourages worker safety we have to begin on a foundation of trust, and fear destroys any chance we have of building trust.

Fear creates an environment and a culture antagonistic to safety in all senses of the word. What's worse is much of the fear that has been institutionalized in organizations has been caused by, or at very least exacerbated by safety professionals themselves. Let's take a look at the

75

five fears:

Fear 1: Fear of Injury or Illness

In 1985, when I joined General Motors as a hardware installer, I was afraid. I had transitioned from a job as a part-time security guard at a nuclear power plant to a highly coveted position in an auto plant. I was poorly trained, and—despite having lived on a farm and worked doing physically demanding work—was not prepared for the rigors of assembly work. Even though OSHA had been around for over a decade my coworkers and I were not required to wear safety glasses (if we wanted them, we had to provide them ourselves) and the cotton gloves provided (absolutely one pair per worker—no exceptions) were wholly inadequate protection against the jagged metal parts I installed. This, coupled with oil-saturated wood-block floors that frequently had blocks missing, minor injuries were a daily occurrence, and back strains, twisted ankles, and other minor injuries were "why we get paid what we do". Unlike some industries where it's considered "tough" or "macho" to ignore injuries, my coworkers and I viewed an injury that required a trip to the medical department as a welcome relief from the back-breaking work that was our jobs. That's not to say that we wanted to get hurt, in fact, we did a good job of looking out for each other and prided ourselves in watching each other's back. We'd complain about unsafe working conditions (blocks in the floor that were missing, frayed electrical cords, or heat that sometimes rose above 140 degrees.) Some supervisors tried to help, but most knew that nothing would be done and would roll their eyes at the complaints. One day an electrician to whom I was casually acquainted died when the afternoon supervisor energized the line on which he was working (he had started at the end of the day shift) electrocuted him. Back then we didn't know or care about Lock Out/Tag Out we counted on communicating to keep us safe.

For many of us, we knew that it was probably only a matter of time before we got hurt, but what were we supposed to do, quit? For blue-collar workers growing up in the 1970's in Detroit, this was the only life for which we were prepared or wanted. Shut up, do your job, and if you beat the odds you came home whole. We knew we were rolling the dice every time we went to work, but we also knew we'd be rolling the dice anywhere we worked so we might as well roll them working for the Big Three, where, at the very least the United Auto Workers could get us great pay, good benefits, and some measure of safety. We didn't talk about it, but the fear was always there. I know that there are some of you reading this and are thinking how much things have changed since that time, and a lot HAS changed. But if you think that fear of injury isn't rampant in the workforce today, you are deluded. As Deming pointed out, no one can really have his or her head in the game when they are terrified that said head might be separated from his or her body in an industrial accident. (I'm paraphrasing Deming, but I think he would agree with my conclusions).

Fear 2: Fear of Write Up

In many workplaces in the world today if you get injured you can expect to be disciplined for your clumsy stupidity or your reckless behavior. You will get a stern lecture about how you are lucky to be alive or that your actions didn't injure someone else. You will likely get a warning, and if the behavior that caused your injury is judged to be a pattern you may be suspended or fired. What rational person will report injury under the threat of disciplinary action? Why would I come clean about my culpability in a mishap knowing that the powers that be will use my admissions against me?

Driving this fear out of the organization is the heart and soul of Just Culture, but far too few organizations have adopted anything close to a culture based on justice.

Fear 3: Fear of Layoff

As a general rule, the jobs most likely to injure a worker are those that require significant physical strength and stamina. This means that when the body ages, wears out, or yes, gets damaged, the workers not only face layoffs but a greatly diminished chance of securing employment elsewhere. This fear that one will become obsolete and lose one's job to someone stronger and more fit is omnipresent in today's fiercely competitive labor market. When the Great Recession hit safety professionals expected a glut of fraudulent cases and found, instead, underreporting as workers fearing that an injury would lead to job loss and impede their ability to find employment elsewhere concealed on the job injuries.

Fear 5: Fear of Embarrassment

Generally speaking, people don't intend to get hurt and when they DO get injured the circumstances leading up to the injury aren't exactly praiseworthy. As long as hazards are the subject of whacky photos the fear will persist. Adults fear workplace embarrassment more than they fear being a workplace fatality. Safety professionals must make a concerted effort to drive out this fear of embarrassment; this effort starts by remembering that safety is no joke.

Fear Four: Fear that One Will Be Ostracized

In the name of behavior modification, safety professionals have created an environment where the mistakes of a single worker can cost all others everything from pizza parties to hundreds of dollars in safety bonuses. Now in addition to the physical consequences associated with an injury, workers must fear the wrath of their fellow workers who are deprived rewards because a coworker has been injured.

Driving fear out of the workplace begins and ends with safety. Safety professionals must foster an environment of trust and open and honest communication if we ever hope to drive fear out of the organization and build a culture where safety is valued.

Deming On Safety: Now You Two Play Nice (Point 9)

Deming's ninth point, "Break down barriers between departments. People in research, design, sales, and production must work as a team, to foresee problems of production and in use that may be encountered with the product or service" is another one of Deming's points that really doesn't take much imagination to connect it to safety

Safety has to be about more than just not getting injured, it has to be about making the workplace better WITHOUT sacrificing safety and that takes teamwork. For far too long the safety department has seen itself as somehow removed from the core business and with every consultant on the planet screaming for Operations leadership to cut cost and concentrate on its core business such think is more than just wrong-headed, it is practically suicide.

"Us Versus Them" Conflict

One of the chief sources of destructive conflicts in organizations is the "us versus them" view of the workplace. Nowhere is the better evidence than in the ongoing battle between Safety and Production, Safety versus Engineering, or Safety and Continuous Improvement. Safety has been the policeman for so many decades that it is tough for other areas of the company to see them as anything but obstructionist. Safety for its part often sees the other departments as recklessly pursuing profit with little regard for the safety of the workers. It's a faux dichotomy; nobody really wants to jeopardize lives in favor of profit, and safety doesn't want to shut down the company to eliminate injuries. But "us versus them" conflict has deep roots and can be difficult to overcome.

In many organizations, the Safety function grew out of Human Resources (HR), which in turn, has its roots in personnel. For many years, HR was the rules and write-up department. Operations made the money and HR was always mucking about with new rules. Human Resources has evolved into a highly functioning partner in most companies' success but for some people, the memories of HR throwing up roadblocks without offering alternative solutions run deep. Fairly or unfairly, Safety has been tarred with that same brush and needs to do something about it.

Safety often has little love for Operations, which it sees, as too willing to take reckless chances and put people at risk. It is seldom that Safety sees Operations as evil or as having malicious intent; it's just that it sees Operations as less than realistic about the likelihood of an injury.

The rift between Safety and Engineering can run almost as deep. Engineering changes to a process, that is, in production tend to be costly and difficult to implement, and even the most carefully designed processes often need to be tweaked after they have been built and installed. Safety professionals rightly expect Engineering to design a safe and capable process, but Engineers aren't always able to "engineer-out" every hazard. Engineering often sees Safety professionals as showing up with objections without solutions—Safety professionals tell Engineering what they CAN'T do without offering viable, safer, alternatives. For their parts, Safety professionals counter that an unsafe design is an unsafe design and it is not their responsibility to design a safe system, rather its job is to identify issues and provide guidance as to whether or not a system is safe.

Perhaps the most bitter—and surprising—rivalry is between Safety and Continuous Improvement. This conflict is part "us versus them" and part "territoriality". It's not surprising that there would be considerable overlap between the two groups. Both functions can rightly claim that activities like 5S (6S to the masters of the obvious who realize that "safety" also begins with an "S" and have renamed the activity); it's little things like this that make the Continuous Improvement professionals roll their eyes when the Safety professionals open their mouths. Safety, on the other hand, resents the CI team referring to them as "non-value added" activity. Many Continuous Improvement groups eye Safety greedily and whisper in the ear of Operations leadership that Safety should reside within the umbrella of CI. Safety, views CI as working too hard to make process improvements without considering the impact changes can have downstream in the process.

Can't We All Just Get Along?

As Deming points out, all activities must work as a team, to "foresee problems of production and in use that may be encountered with the product or service". If worker injuries, overexposure that causes industrial illnesses, or fatalities don't represent a problem that will interfere with production, it is difficult to envision one that would. But how can an organization break down these barriers? Sometimes the simplest solutions are the best:

Co-located Teams. Conventional wisdom holds that functions should sit together, after all, doesn't it make sense that everyone in a functional department would sit together. Unfortunately, teams that aren't housed together (in some organizations, an individual might never have met his or her program manager in person, interacting only on conference calls and via email.) Co-located teams (those where members are seated with their project teams instead of their functions) tend to be more cohesive and higher functioning than other teams.

Goal-Based Compensation. It may surprise some to learn that many team members are compensated dramatically different than their colleagues from different functions. As long as one function can be successful while the other fails there is a strong danger of creating destructive competition and conflict. Cross-functional teams should be given a common goal and compensated according to how effectively they achieved it.

Cross-Training and Interdisciplinary Rotations. The best way to understand and value a teammate's contribution to the team is to walk the proverbial mile his or her shoes. A greater understanding of how each function operates is key to closer working relationships. Cross training or a rotation to a different function can greatly improve the level of cooperation between groups.

Not every Safety function is at odds with other functions (this is the kind of disclaimer I have to put in because despite my earnest belief that my readers are smart enough to distinguish between me identifying a problem and not weaseling it up by qualifying each statement with a "many" "few" or similar verbal marshmallows some half-wit inevitably stumbles across my post and hammers out a frothy "I hate you" email) but those who fail to reach a high degree of collaboration with traditional rivals will likely go the way of the dinosaur.

Deming on Safety: Point Ten

> Deming's tenth point—"Eliminate slogans, exhortations, and targets for the workforce asking for zero defects and new levels of productivity. Such exhortations only create adversarial relationships, as the bulk of the causes of low quality and low productivity belong to the system and thus lie beyond the power of the workforce."—is particularly applicable to safety.

Since the inception of the safety function, organizations have been festooning the walls with platitude after platitude, and what's more, advocates of Behavior-Based Safety (BBS) often encourage these exhortations in the name of safety awareness. This point, above all of Deming's 14 points, is likely to draw criticisms from safety professionals.   I've already addressed the need to eliminate "zero injuries" as a slogan or a goal, so I won't revisit the topic here. Key to Deming's tenth point is the last part of the statement. Deming believed that campaigns that promote improvements in quality or productions ultimately led to hard feelings, low morale and an adversarial relationship between workers and management, and even between workers themselves. If Deming's view can be accepted than safety slogans, campaigns, and targets not only don't work, but they actually impede safety.

I've long known that slogans, posters, and other things that remind people not to die quickly fade into the landscape of the workplace. People become "normal blind" to not only to the posters and slogans, but to the hazards in the workplace as well. As workers acclimate to their surroundings the elements of the environment that are ever present become part of their subconscious. Posters telling people to work safe may make the organization feel as if it is doing something, but for the most part it does little more than provide the safety function some small comfort. But after writing and speaking about safety, and consistently condemning this practice I recognize that the safety professionals who love this practice would rather die than abandon this silly and pointless activity.

What I find most intriguing is the very last sentence of Deming's tenth point. To apply Deming's tenth point, safety professionals have to accept that "the bulk of the causes of (injuries) belong to the system and thus lie beyond the power of the workforce." This is a tough sell for most safety professionals—as it was for quality and operations professionals when Deming first proffered the idea. When the National Safety Council announced finding that over 90% of all injuries were caused by unsafe behavior nobody questioned it. An entire industry that sold variation on a theme: reward safe behavior and discourage risky behavior and the workplace will become safer.

But what if Deming was right? What if most safety issues are the fault of the system and not, because of careless, mouth-breathing imbeciles who just won't be careful, as so many seem to believe? What if people get hurt because of system flaws and NOT because they are cocky jerks that take unnecessary risks? I happen to believe that nobody wants to get hurt, and in general, people don't knowingly and deliberate endanger others by taking stupid or reckless risks. I don't do these things and I bet you don't do them either. Are the people we are charged with protecting that different from us? Why would we assume that everyone in the world accept us is stupid, reckless, or evil?

After years of working in both continuous improvement and worker safety I have come to believe that most injuries are caused by unsafe behaviors, BUT most unsafe behaviors are caused by poorly designed, or poorly performing, systems. The real question lies in whether or not workers (or for that matter, safety professionals) can do anything meaningful to correct unsafe behaviors without first and foremost correcting the system flaws that create or reward the behaviors.

It took years for quality and operations professionals to accept that placing the onus for defects and productivity bottle necks on the workers was counter-productive and even harmful (Deming published his 14 points decades before it became common practice in world-class manufacturing, and many denounced him as overly academic, deluded, or just plain wrong.) The principle difference between Deming advocating a change in how quality and productivity are managed and safety professionals advocating for a change in how safety is viewed is that when people resisted Deming they had quality defects and stubborn bottlenecks, but when people resist changes to safety they risk killing people in the plants.

Safety as an industry is dangerously addicted to Behavior Based Safety. The giants of the safety industry essentially all have the same business model: collect fees for certifying safety professionals in their methodologies, wait for the safety professionals who are so certified to spread like cancer through the industry, and sell training materials, posters, slogans, and sundry crap to keep the pyramid scheme alive. One personality in particular continues making a good living retelling (both in live speeches and via video tapes) in gruesome detail, the story of how his own careless behavior and short cuts caused his horrific injuries. While his story is poignant and compelling, how does it help someone in a similar situation? In fact, this person's situation (I've sat through at least a dozen presentations over the years) illustrates Deming's points nicely. As he engaged in unsafe behaviors, did he assess the risks before he took the shortcuts and determine that the rewards were worth taking? Or is it more likely that he engaged in behavior he had done scores—if not hundreds or thousands of times? People love a good horror story, and this is no exception, but aside from the questionable entertainment value, what good does it do to have workers listen to a maudlin retelling of a series of mistakes. The message, "it can happen to you" generally falls on deaf ears. For every behavior cited in that story I can point to three system problems that would have to be corrected to prevent a similar issue from injuring workers in the future.

Deming's tenth point really applies to a series of lessons for safety.

First, safety slogans and targets don't work—at least as it applies to lowering injuries. Next, programs aimed at achieving safety goals are just as likely to impede safety as they are to improve things, and finally, it's wrong to expect workers to bear the primary responsibility for reducing injuries when the causes for the vast majority of injuries lie outside the average worker's ability to correct them.

Deming On Safety Point 11

"Eliminate arbitrary numerical targets: Eliminate work standards that prescribe quotas for the work force and numerical goals for people in management. Substitute aids and helpful leadership in order to achieve continual improvement of quality and productivity."—W. Edward Deming's 11th point; presents safety professionals with something of a quandary. After all, we have been told for decades that we can't improve without goals, but what acceptable goal can have we except zero injuries. This point is probably the most misunderstood thing Deming ever wrote. His position is not anti-measurement and goals; it's against the checklist mentality where managers can't see beyond the idea of pushing out production at all costs. In writing this point, Deming was saying that organizations need to stop counting things that really don't matter and start focusing on making the process more efficient overall. Deming believed that if managers focused on proactively making the process better the numbers would take care of themselves.

Safety professionals can learn a lot from this point. We have got to stop counting bodies and congratulating ourselves for "good" safety records because we kill less than our competitors or we achieved the dubious honor of maiming and crippling less workers than industry average. Instead of counting the grizzly "butcher's bill" (as the English Navy used to informally refer to casualties) safety professionals should be actively moving to a continuous improvement approach.

Deming wasn't condemning lagging indicators, rather he was saying we shouldn't gauge our success based on these measures. We can't improve without examining both leading and lagging indicators and what I will call predictive measures. Leading indicators show us patterns and suggest areas on which we may want to keep an eye. These measures show us trends and provide clues about what actions we may want to avert injuries. Lagging indicators are important sources of information relative to the effectiveness of our efforts. Leading and lagging indicators are only truly useful when examined together (what do we need to do? And how effective have our efforts been to date?)

But there is a third set of indicators with which safety professionals still struggle. I call these predictive measures of risk, or risk indicators if you prefer. Risk indicators are those things—typically esoteric to a given facility—that are known to raise the risk of injuries, typically for a short duration. These risk indicators include things like part shortages, absenteeism, overtime, nonstandard work, etc. Risk indicators are tough to operationally define across an industry or even, in many cases, across a single organization. I suppose one could argue that risk indicators are a subcategory of leading indicators, but I would discourage you from lumping them together with leading indicators, because one should be managing these two types of data differently. As I stated, leading indicators should work in tandem with lagging indicators, the analysis is essentially an exercise in determining if what you thought would happen in the future is confirmed by what happened in the past. Risk indicators are happening in the present and while we may respond to them in much the same way as we would to a leading indicator, our actions are much more urgent in the case of risk indicators. But don't get too hung up on the semantics; what's important is that there is more to managing safety indicators than making counts.

Following Deming's advice to refocus manager's attention toward continuous improvement of the process will take more effort than many organizations realize. For starters, many managers lack even the most basic understanding of worker safety, the true causes of injuries, the relationship between injuries and operating costs or efficiency, and what our cherished safety statistics mean. We have tried for so long to make ourselves seem so smart and to mystify our profession that we have succeeded in being seen as outsiders. If we are to expect managers to change the way they view worker safety we must be prepared to step in with tools, training, and real help in translating all the gobbledygook that we take for granted into real, useful, and practical information. These days, most managers are feeling overwhelmed, overworked, and over committed to results over which they have very little input.

This uncovers another, much more serious problem. Many safety professionals are ill-equipped to interpret data and extrapolate the best response to what the data is telling them. Few safety professionals are expert in data analysis, statistics, or in some cases even the basic business of the larger organization. When one feels out of one's league, and in over one's head, one tends to gravitate to the familiar and in this case, the familiar is numerical counts.

To further complicate things, we need numerical counts. Unlike quality, governments require us to provide injury counts (although adjusted for hours worked LWDI, DART, and Incident rates are still essentially quantitative data). And it's not just governments that require us to use numerical counts insurance companies base our premiums on quantitative data. Here in lies the problem, for decades organizations have tried to repurpose this data inappropriately. We may have to report these figures, but we don't have to manage against it. At its essence, that's what Deming's 11th point is saying, "stop using quantitative data in situations where qualitative data is more appropriate. In other words, stop comparing yourself to industry average, stop exhausting your resources trying to report what happened and instead, focus your efforts on keeping it from happening in the future. I think what Deming was trying to convey here, is that organizations get so wrapped up in the (fairly pointless) details and stop seeing the forest amid all those trees.

Until we stop bureaucratically counting bodies and start looking for ways to stop hurting workers instead, we will be caught in a vicious circle of hurt-measure-kill.

Deming on Safety Point 12 "Remove Barriers to Pride of Workmanship"

When I first contemplated the relationship of Deming's 12th point (Remove Barriers to Pride of Workmanship. Remove barriers that rob people in management and in engineering of their right to pride of workmanship. This means, inter alia, abolishment of the annual or merit rating and of management by objective") to safety I confess a certain misgiving. At first blush there didn't seem to be a clear parallel and when I sat down to write this series I committed to not drawing connections where none truly existed.

And what, after all, does safety have to do with removing barriers to pride of workmanship? After reflecting on this point, I think not only are their connections between this point and safety, but these connections are pronounced and profound.

First, there is an implied call to remove the barriers that rob people of their rights and responsibilities to think for themselves. At the heart of the pride of workmanship is the understanding that as the worker, you have created something remarkable, you have done something that is an extension of yourself, and you have done something enduring and worthwhile. For one to accomplish these things, one must have the authority to make the choices that shape the work. I don't believe that it's too much of a stretch to apply these same sentiments to safety, and it's essential that we do.

If we truly believe that safety is everyone's job, then we cannot prevent workers from making their own decisions as they relate to safety. There are many barriers to the kind of pride of workmanship that relates to safety, with the safety professional chief among them.

Often, in their zeal, safety professionals throw so many rules at Operations that to follow them would paralyze Operations and choke productivity. Faced with these choices, workers are forced to guess which rule can safely be broken.

Many times, workers are forced to follow rules which make no sense or that seemingly contradict common sense. Since the worker has no say in the construction of safety regulations he or she can take no ownership of the rule or show any pride in ensuring compliance with it. Of course, not all safety regulations are negotiable or even universally applicable. Government's routinely dictate safety regulations to us and we have no choice in how we comply. That having been said, it is completely possible and appropriate to include workers in discussions regarding how best to comply with the regulation without hamstringing the worker's ability to efficiently to the tasks.

Secondarily, there are still huge pockets within industry that insist on managing safety by objectives and that routinely provide incentives for injury-free workdays. Obviously, there is a perfect correlation between this element of the twelfth point and the world of safety. Organizations must stop the practice of managing safety by objectives and rewarding people for the absence of injuries instead of the presence of safety, i.e. lowering the probability of injury to the lowest praticible levels.

Deming on Safety: The 13th Point"

Deming's 13th point— "Institute education and self-improvement"—
is near and dear to me. Long before I began my career in safety, I
worked in organizational development and training. My degree is in
adult education (it sounds dirty, but it really isn't) and I have always
enjoyed and am passionate about training. Before we continue, I
should make it clear that there is a difference between "education" and
"training". Education is teaching someone about something, while
training is teaching them to do something. So, while you might
support sex education of elementary school children you probably
don't support sex training of this same population.

What Deming understood about process improvement is that much of
the efficiency, accuracy, and quality of the process is dependent on
human behavior and that such behavior is intrinsically unpredictable.
But through education (and Deming uses this term to describe what
should rightly be called training) and self-improvement workers are
better prepared to meet the challenges associated with their jobs. The
connection between education and safety is as strong as the one Deming
pointed to between education and quality.

I have said many times that the best investment in worker safety is a
solid training program—not just in safety—but in the core skills as well.
Workers who understand the "how's" and "whys" of their job are far
better prepared to work safely than those whose training has been less
formal, poorly designed, and amateurishly delivered.

Apart from training in the core skills and safety, workers greatly benefit from training in problem-solving skills. Workers with strong problem-solving skills are able to devise process improvements that also improve worker safety. Kaizen skills are essentially specialized problem-solving skills. Problem-solving is the essence of injury investigation, where workers must understand the big picture and look for multiple lines of causation.

Another key skill set that is essential for preventing workplace injuries is stress management. Stress contributes to injuries in several ways. First, it interferes with people's decision making and people who are under a great deal of stress are far more likely to make poor choices (and suffer the injuries associated with those poor decisions. Stress also causes physical illnesses, and while much of our work is focused on injury prevention, it behooves us to remember that we are also responsible (well most of are) with worker health. Finally, stress contributes to human error as one of a number of "performance shaping" factors that raise the probability that someone will make an unconscious or inadvertent error that contributes to an injury.

The organization should train all workers in its core business. Workers need to understand how the company makes money and how it competes. This understanding of the core goals of the corporation will make all operations run more efficiently, and efficient processes don't hurt workers.

Self-improvement need not be limited to intellectual pursuits. Keeping oneself in sufficient physical condition to meet the rigors of the job is also an important part of self-improvement. Workers who lack good cardio health, lack stamina because of excess weight or are in poor health because of their lifestyles should be encouraged (not forced, mind you) to maintain a healthy physique.

But Deming's point that organizations need to institute education and self-improvement program is more than developing training, it's about developing a strategy and this exercise is as important to worker safety as it is to quality. Continuing to hone worker skills will help the workers to be better prepared to make safer decisions and to build true resilience.

93

Deming didn't think a lot about safety, at least if he did, his work doesn't reflect it. To Deming, process inefficiency needed to be approached holistically—process waste in whatever form (defects, bottlenecks, or injuries)—could be managed effectively using most of the same tactics. In other words, it's not that Deming didn't care about safety, rather, he didn't see safety as an external element of a well-managed business.

Deming on Safety Point 14: The Transformation is Everyone's Job

> By far the most universal belief in worker safety is that safety is impossible without top management commitment and action. It's also the most offered excuse for the failure of a safety management system. I don't think I have ever attended a safety conference where I didn't run into at least one caterwauling, simpering, burnt-out safety professional who blamed all his failures on a lack of support from leadership, or management.

Too many safety professionals are orphans of the modern workplace; helpless eunuchs who are afraid to do their jobs. In most cases, the safety professional is both leader and management. What's worse is that they don't want their jobs to get better; they would rather have sympathy. Too many safety professionals would rather stand on the sidelines and grouse that the game is fixed and they have been cheated than to get in the game and win.

Deming believed that organizational transformation was everyone's job; that everyone in the organization played an integral role in moving the organization away from outdated methodologies and obsolete values and toward a high-functioning organization that is capable of competing on a global scale.

Deming was big on vision but offered little in instruction as to exactly how we are supposed to achieve the desired state. A lot of people criticize him for that, but I think Deming's lack of prescriptive tools is the greatest manifestation of his genius. There is no magic bullet in business, and there is no one solution that every organization can implement that will guarantee success. Ideas need to be adapted to the business conditions of each individual organization and environments. And while there is no magic recipe for transforming a corporate culture, here are some general guidelines for exactly who owns what in cultural transformation.

Top Management Commitment and Action

This step resonates with safety professionals who desperately want operations leadership to assume ownership of safety. Certainly, senior leadership must be committed to an efficient and safe workplace. If the C-suite doesn't value safety, then safety cannot exist. Unfortunately, many senior leaders don't have a clue as to exactly what it means to transform the workplace into one that values safety. This issue underscores the on-going need for safety professionals to educate leaders in what they need to do to achieve true workplace safety. It's unfair for safety professionals to expect management support and commitment until they provide, in specific, measurable terms exactly what their goals and methods are, and the tasks necessary to achieve them.

Transformation of Safety

The definition of insanity is doing the same thing over and over and expecting a different result. This idiom nicely describes many in safety. If we are going to transform our organizations into high-functioning, highly effective organizations that value worker safety as essential to business excellence then perhaps the biggest transformation must come in the safety professionals themselves. It's time to re-engineer safety— scrape away all the fads, the vestigial practices based on junk science, and commit to change. Changing the safety professional begins in academia. We need to stop producing generation after generation of safety professionals who are trained to perpetuate safety superstitions based on eighty-year-old research. We could quickly add safety professional organizations to this list of institutions in need of transformation. Professional conferences must stop pandering to the safety of demagogues and hucksters who gather to tell each other what they already believe. The safety media has to stop buckling to safety vendors who, in many cases, dictate which stories are permitted in print (and before anyone accuses me of bellyaching, I have never had a story squelched because of an advertiser, but I have been asked to tone down my rhetoric a bit in response to an advertiser complaint.) I will leave it to you to decide if I did.

Operations

Operations must invest in core skills training and stop pressuring the training function for less time spent in classrooms. Training remains the single best way to improve workplace safety, and yet Operations often fights to get workers back into production quicker. This is short-sighted; studies have shown that there is a direct correlation between quality worker training and workplace productivity and worker safety. Operations must come to realize that there is no such thing as profitability and profits without safety.

Maintenance

Poorly maintained facilities and equipment are significant sources of workplace risk. Unfortunately, too often, the maintenance and facilities departments are given passes for not meeting their obligations for worker safety. All maintenance and facility managers need do is howl that they don't have enough resources and too often senior leadership lets them off the hook. Lack of resources is not an excuse for not containing a hazard. While it is often impossible to correct a hazard, it is seldom impossible, or even prohibitive to contain a hazard using low-cost alternatives.

Purchasing

Too often purchasing does not look beyond cost. Buying equipment, tools, machines, and materials without taking the safety of these items into consideration often undermines the overall safety of the workplace. In some cases, an investment in purchased goods that are safer to work with and operate will pay off significantly by creating a safer work environment.

Continuous Improvement

In many organizations, the continuous improvement group is completely removed and independent from the Safety function. This organization needs to change quickly if the company is to steward its resources and to improve safety through process improvements. The internecine rivalries between Safety and CI are destructive and should be sought out and exterminated.

Deming was right. Transformation IS everyone's job and transforming the organization to one that values worker safety and sees safety as an integral element in workplace efficiency will require unprecedented cooperation between traditional rivals. The work will be hard, but the benefits will make this work worth the effort.

CHAPTER 4

My Problem with Pyramids

Deming on Safety Point 14: The Transformation is Everyone's Job

Heinrich's Pyramid has been a boil in the inner ear of safety since its inception. Two parts fiction and one-part bigotry against non-Aryan races, one would have thought that this rubbish born of shoddy research, bigoted beliefs that workers got hurt mostly because they were of lesser breeding than good upstanding white protestants, and a lazy researcher who may or may not have made the whole conclusion up would have quickly been dismissed by smart Safety practitioners. But the problem is...people love statistics, even ones that are made up. I once posted "63% of all statistics are made up" and one outraged dimwit demanded that I provide him the source. And while there is now some doubt that P.T. Barnum never actually said, "there's a sucker born every minute" I'm pretty sure he would like that people credit him with saying it—especially if he didn't. Never has this axiom ever been truer than in the faint hearts and weak minds of people who cling to this pyramid like a Pitbull with a Pomeranian in its jaws.

Over the years, I have challenged safety practitioners to view safety differently, to see beyond the fads, the snake oil, and to see safety for what it is, the product of well-managed business practices in the areas of competency, process capability, hazard and risk management, accountability systems, and engagement. I have explored competency and process capability and this week I will take a close look at hazard and risk management.

This topic is by far the most difficult to explore, not because it's not well understood, but because it is so frequently misunderstood. So many of the basic tenets of safety—when done correctly—support this business element. Unfortunately, so few of these things are done correctly.

Take for example Heinrich's insufferable pyramid. Safety practitioners all over the world still trot out Heinrich's Pyramid as proof positive that if you have x number of near misses you will have y number of serious injuries and z number of fatalities. Safety practitioners cling to this concept like a tick on the soft white underbelly of business. But Heinrich's Pyramid is a steaming pile of crap. Forget that evidence suggest that he may have made his evidence up, forget that no serious researchers (those who don't collect checks for perpetuating this garbage) believe there is any statistical validity to the pyramid, and forget that Heinrich himself admitted that his research itself consisted of asking 1920's front-line supervisors how injuries happened ten years or so after they actually happened. Forget all that. The greatest flaw in Heinrich's Pyramid is that we never really know how many near misses, minor injuries, or unsafe acts there are, so effectively we are missing half the information we need to make any meaningful inferences. But there I go again spoiling things for the safety professionals who: a) don't give a rat's testicle whether or not the pyramid is valid and b) are too lazy to replace it with something more meaningful.

Of course, on the other side of the spectrum, we have those who hate Heinrich with the venom and vitriol of the people who hate Heinrich Himmler. This school of thought holds that everything that Heinrich believed is wrong and damaging to the safety organization. These people, I believe, are throwing the baby out with the bathwater. While there is no value in trying to predict the expected number of injuries using Heinrich's Pyramid, there is value to using the pyramid as an analogy to better help Operations value the benefit of correcting hazards. When forced (which is too often) to incorporate insipid pyramid into a training I am developing or presenting I explain it by saying that we know that for every injury there are numerous hazards that could have harmed us but didn't, close calls, or minor injuries. We may not be able to use that to predict the number of future injuries but a heck of a lot of hazards represent a heck of a lot of potential for harm. That's it, no hackneyed lectures about behavior.

Maybe the better analogy would be of an iceberg. The area above the waterline would be the reported injuries, recordables, DART Injuries, and fatalities and below the waterline would be the hazards, unreported minor injuries, and risk conditions. The point is that if we focus on the hazards before people get hurt we end up reducing the iceberg both above and below the waterline.

Managing hazards is pretty simple (which I'll bet dollars to doughnuts is the reason so many safety practitioners hate it): find the hazards, contain the hazards, and track the hazard to its permanent correction. Of course, implementing this simple process isn't easy but making it more complex doesn't make it any easier.

Managing hazards begins with identifying hazards and the best way to do that is to walk the work area and look for things that can hurt people. We don't need to worry about whether or not the hazard is a physical condition or the result of an ancient curse, or the act of an avenging pagan god. This is not to say that we shouldn't investigate the causes, but we need to stop obsessing and finding profundity in the ordinary.

Once we have found a hazard we must be sure that we don't walk away from it without containing it. There is more than just the obvious reason (because someone could get hurt before we get around to it) there are legal liability issues to consider if you find and document a hazard but fail to contain (and record the containment) a hazard.

Tracking the hazard to completion adds another layer to the hazard management process and it provides real value. Meeting weekly to discuss the progress toward correcting hazards helps to build ownership among Operations, it makes the previously invisible visible and applies coercive force on the people responsible for getting things fixed (who often sweep fixing hazards aside for sexier work).

Keeping it simple is an easier sell to the organization than some complex mumbo-jumbo.

Correcting hazards tends to return more on the effort than just reducing injuries. Because we eliminate the root causes of system failures, we likely will eliminate other process bottlenecks that affect cost, quality, delivery, and morale.

The Power of Pyramids: How Using Outmoded Thinking About Hazards Can Be Deadly

Gallons of virtual ink have been used in writings condemning Heinrich's Pyramid. But even though a significant population in the safety industry question its validity not only does the malarkey still persist, it thrives. What's more, people believe accept it as a universal truth in industries where Heinrich had no standing.

Throughout my storied career as an organizational change agent and safety strategy consultant, I've met with resistance in the form of "that won't work here, we're not..." fill in the blank. Whether it be Mining, Oil & Gas, Chemicals, Aerospace, Heavy Truck, the Entertainment Industry, Construction, Healthcare or Logistics the first time I worked in those industries (and yes, I have actually WORKED in those industries) I was met by this objection. Early on I believed that the objection was absolute hogwash but eventually came around to a way of thinking that caused me to stop hawking my one-size-fits-all solution in favor of co-designed and co-developed, shaped interventions that consider the challenges of a given client culture, geographic location, industry, and even site. The solutions tailored to the specific needs of a customer are universally better (or at least as good) as something that the safety conglomerates and mom-and-pop snake oil salesmen have been successfully selling for decades. I even defend this in another blog post In Defense of Not-Invented-Here-Thinking.

If executives in Oil & Gas, Mining, Energy, and Construction et al, rightfully believe that other safety tools and methodologies are not necessarily applicable to their worlds why are they so quick to drink the Heinrich Kool-Aid? Before I answer that, I guess I should provide a bit of background information.

For the uninitiated, Herbert William Heinrich was an American statistician who in the late 1920's and early 1930s studied worker safety in an industrial setting (specifically manufacturing) He created a pyramid based on his "law" that for every accident that causes a major injury, there are 29 accidents that cause minor injuries and 300 accidents that cause no injuries. He arranged it in a neat little pyramid and claimed that because many accidents share common root causes, addressing more commonplace accidents that cause no injuries can prevent accidents that cause injuries. He also found that more than 80% of all injuries were caused by unsafe behaviors. It makes sense which is what makes it so dangerous.

Heinrich's Pyramid became a mainstay of safety theory and was largely unquestioned for 80 years or so until Fred A. Manuele reviewed Heinrich's "research" and found real problems with it. Like Heinrich, Manuele retired from the insurance industry albeit many years later. In his book, Heinrich Revisited: Truisms or Myths, Manuele openly called much of Heinrich's work into question, specifically:

No one seems able to find Heinrich's files on his original research making it impossible to peer review (and is accepted practice in scientific research today) impossible. This doesn't necessarily mean that Heinrich wasn't spot on, but it does mean that we can never know how he came up with his conclusions and ultimately if there is any scientific or statistical validity to his work. We would never accept these conclusions from a researcher today just because they "sound reasonable".

Heinrich's studied accidents that happened in the 1920s, in a manufacturing environment that bears little to no resemblance to the workplace of today.

Heinrich placed a disproportionate emphasis on psychology which impeded his ability to remain impartial. Heinrich asserted that psychology was "a fundamental of great importance in accident causation". In other words, Heinrich saw exactly what he expected and even wanted to see. He was selling hammers and the whole world looked like a nail. It's just like optometrists; if you go to one you will most likely get told that you need glasses.

The methodology Heinrich used to generate his pyramid ratios cannot be supported. In Manuele's considered, and expert, opinion "Current causation knowledge indicates the premise to be invalid." Manuele also pointed out that the "premise conflicts with the work of others, such as W. Edwards Deming, whose research finds root causes to derive from shortcomings in the management systems."

Fred Manuele suffered greatly for his work. The mouth breathing behavior freaks attacked him and his work personally and professionally, and yet he persisted. In his, Reviewing Heinrich: Dislodging Two Myths from the Practice of Safety, Fred A. Manuele systematically analyzes Heinrich's work and calls into question two of the most cherished beliefs in the safety community: 1) that most injuries are caused by unsafe acts and 2) that reducing the frequency of injuries will automatically reduce the severity of injuries.

But enough about that, flogging this dead horse will only get me hate mail and death threats from the current freakshow of BBS zealots and I have neither the time nor the patience for that. Let's just assume that you mouth-breathers and snake oil salesmen hate me and would like to see me dead. Get in line. My ex-wife has started a club you can join.

If Heinrich's Pyramid is so deeply flawed why are so many executives so enamored of it? Simple:

1. We taught them this. There aren't many MBA programs that teach how to manage worker safety, and the captains of industry rely on safety professionals to provide them with the basic information they need to know to be successful. So many safety pundits, snake oil salesmen, and BBS fanatics have taught this dreck as Gospel that it has

become accepted.

2.   It makes sense. Like so many myths and urban legends the idea that reducing minor injuries and OSHA recordables will ultimately reduce severe injuries and fatalities stands to reason. But just like so many myths and urban legends, this assertion ignores some key information. For the pyramid to make sense each hazard would have to have an equal potential to kill as it does to cause a minor injury and that just isn't true. Let me give you an example. Smoking near a concentration of flammable gas is a) highly likely to cause an injury and b) that injury is highly likely to be deadly. Using a crescent wrench to complete a task that requires a pipe wrench can cause an injury, but that injury is far more likely to be a minor first aid case than it is to kill someone. Unless your safety management system has a good way of distinguishing between high risk hazards capable of killing multiple workers (and perhaps members of your surrounding communities) from those that are going require a band-aid and a kiss on the boo-boo from a sympathetic health care provider you create a system where you give the same urgency and attention to a life-threatening hazard that you do to a benign condition.

3.   It places the burden on workers to work more safely. How many times have you thought, "if these idiots would just be more careful they wouldn't keep getting hurt?" Don't beat yourself up for thinking it, heck we all do at some point or another. Blaming the injured worker makes us feel better. It absolves us of the blame for not having done more to prevent the injury and protect the worker. If we emphasize on behavior and individual responsibility instead of finding and fixing system flaws and improving decision-making skills, then we can sleep better at night. But what's more the belief that it's all about behavior has created a cottage industry of safety incentives, based on the notion that people will take safety more seriously if there is money on the line. Incentives work, unfortunately, more often than not the incentive is to commit fraud by not reporting a legitimate work injury so as not to jeopardize a reward for no injuries.

Okay fine, but is this really putting workers at risk? You betcha:

- It creates a false sense of safety. Too many people believe that the organization working the bottom of the pyramid is actually creating meaningful results and lowering the risk of injuries. They will proudly point to a significant reduction in injuries as proof that they have slain the injury dragon. Until someone dies. And then someone else dies. And so on until the company breaks out in a cold sweat as the "who's next?" climate of fear takes hold.

- It relies on information that you can't effectively or completely gather. Even if we discount the criticisms of the validity of the pyramid's ratios the bottom of the pyramid (near misses and unsafe conditions) cannot ever be accurately calculated. How many physical hazards go unnoticed? How many unsafe behaviors happen day in and day out but are never identified? And how many near misses go unreported? Furthermore, the information that most companies are able to gather on first aid cases is equally dubious because many workers will treat minor injuries with a quick trip to the first aid kit.

- It overwhelms safety systems. Many well-intentioned safety practitioners actively seek to gather good information on non-recordable injuries only to quickly become immersed in a nightmare of data. Again, because attempts to collect information on hazards and near misses (working the bottom of the pyramid) often lack a means of prioritizing hazards the organization becomes a bureaucratic quagmire of useless data points instead of actionable information.

- It isn't equally applicable across industry segments, countries, locations, or sites. Hazards are contextual. Without both interaction and a catalyst, the threat of injury from a given hazard is just potential. Welding without a hot work permit is a hazard, but the context can differ wildly and lethally. Is welding without a hot work permit on a muddy construction site the same threat to safety as welding around flammable gas or in a confined space of a mine?

- It promotes overzealous case management. If the number of OSHA recordables is directly proportional to the number of fatalities, then it would be irresponsible (if not criminal) to not use every tool to reduce recordables. One such tool is case management. Unfortunately, while case management can save organizations thousands of dollars and make its safety record seem better than what it actually is; it does nothing to reduce the risk of injuries. So, IF the ratio is valid (it isn't) good case management downplays the risks of fatalities, by seeming to reduce OSHA recordables when it isn't doing anything of substance to actually reduce the risk of a fatality.

As safety professionals we have collectively created this mess and it's our responsibility to clean it up. Here's what we need to do:

1. Admit we were wrong. We have to suck it up and admit that we have been perpetuating nonsense.

2. Re-educate leaders. We taught the leaders to believe that these concepts would apply to every industry, site, and situation. We now need to correct this wrong-headed notion and look for better solutions for our specific situations. It will send the purveyors of snake oil and the BBS zealots into a fever pitch, but we owe it to the workers to correct this mistake.

3. Shift the focus from worker behaviors to leader behaviors. Do you find yourself unwilling to let go of the "unsafe behavior as causation" doctrine? Fine, but recognize that your processes and organization play a major role in WHY people behave as they do and that the leaders have the single greatest influence on the system and worker behavior. Place the blame for unsafe behaviors where it belongs.

I could go on and on (and in fact already have) but the bottom line is this, as long as we persist in perpetuating these myths and promulgating them across industries we increasingly endanger workers.

CHAPTER 5

This Kool Aid Tastes Funny: My Ongoing Battle Against Behavior Based Safety (BBS)

The Basics of Safety: Behavior-Based Safety vs. Process-Based Safety

Originally published in *Fabricating & Metalworking Magazine,* it can be found here: http://www.fabricatingandmetalworking.com/2012/11/the-basics-of-safetybehavior-based-safety-vs-process-based-safety/2/

> Exploring why the widest gulf between safety philosophies lies between these two of the more popular systematic approaches.

Behavior-Based Safety, or BBS as it is often called, is an approach to worker safety based on a combination of behavioral science research, organizational behavior, and behavioral psychology. In broad strokes, BBS is based upon the idea that the vast majority of injuries are caused by unsafe acts and the safety of the workplace can be significantly improved by activities aimed at reinforcing safe behaviors and raising the awareness of unsafe acts.

There are many different BBS systems and the popularity of the methodology has grown exponentially in recent years. The system is particularly attractive among business owners and safety professionals that are frustrated by a pattern of injuries that could have been easily prevented had the injured parties simply exercised a modicum of care. BBS systems seek to impart accountability for safety to workers while encouraging safe behavior through feedback and incentives.

While much recent research has been done supporting BBS systems, many of the basic concepts are rooted in the work of early behavior and industrial psychologists, most notably Fredrick Taylor and Herbert

Heinrich. In 1911 Fredrick Taylor published his seminal work, The Principles of Scientific Management, which advocated the use of the scientific method in managing workers to improve productivity. Scientific management techniques promoted standardizing work around the optimization of jobs to the point where workers could be taught and managed against a single standard way of doing the job. These scientific techniques eventually evolved into the discipline of industrial engineering.

In 1926 Hebert Heinrich, while working at the Travelers Insurance company, published Incidental Cost of Accidents to the Employer. In this and subsequent works, he concluded that the vast majority of injuries were caused by controllable unsafe actions.

The Behavior-Based Safety philosophies grew from the belief derived from these and other bodies of work that the best way to reduce injuries is to modify the behaviors that are most likely to cause those injuries. Over time, however, there have risen numerous BBS methodologies and practitioners that do not always agree on the optimum formula for affecting behavioral change, even though their systems typically share these three commonalities:

Promotion of Awareness. A workplace that is heavily invested in BBS is likely to employ numerous visual tools designed to remind workers of the importance of working safely and to encourage workers to be mindful of the consequences for not working safely. One especially popular promotion is the incorporation of posters drawn by the children of the workers, underscoring the impact that a serious injury will have beyond the workplace.

Incentives. BBS proponents believe that providing incentives for working safe plays an important part of any safety system. Incentives for working safely can range from simple financial bonuses for a specified period where no workers were injured to complex safety games and contests with elaborate prizes.

Safety Observations. In safety observations, an experienced worker –

113

typically a supervisor or safety professional – will watch a worker do his or her job, after which the observer provides feedback on the safety with which the worker completed the job. The point of observing the work being performed is to point out unsafe acts and offer tips for making the job safer.

Behavior-Based Safety is not without critics. Perhaps the harshest critics deride BBS for blaming the victim and contend that BBS is little more than a means of pitting workers against one another. These critics contend that because workers do not actually want to get hurt, then penalizing them for getting hurt by withholding a bonus literally adds insult to injury.

Many critics describe the techniques used to raise awareness as condescending. As one frustrated worker described it, "they give us a pizza party once a week if we don't kill anyone." The worker went on to complain that management acted as if the only reason workers were concerned about safety was the prospect of reward.

In some poorly executed BBS programs, incentives were shown to decrease incident reporting rather than reducing actual injuries. The pressure to conceal job-related injuries can be profound. With coworkers facing the loss of everything from Safety BINGO game pieces to bonuses of $500 or more, an injured worker has a very real incentive to conceal the injury. It is not unheard of for a worker to seek medical attention at his or her own expense to avoid a recordable because the cost of treatment is far less than amount forfeited in the loss of a bonus.

Still, others will acknowledge the effectiveness of a BBS system but argue that the cost of observations, data analysis, and the significant safety infrastructure needed to sustain the gains achieved by BBS are far more than is necessary or practical.

All of these criticisms are hotly contested by BBS proponents who point to reams of research that support their methodologies, but critics counter that research conducted by individuals with a financial stake in the findings is intrinsically unreliable. Some critics focus on a more basic position: that the level of variability in human behavior is so great that any attempt to manipulate it on a system scale is unrealistic and impossible.

Even the harshest critics begrudgingly agree that the largest contributor to injuries cannot be ignored. But what lies at the heart of the conflict is whether the root cause of workplace injuries is deliberate behavior or the processes and systems that encourage bad decision-making. In either case, most safety professionals will agree that behavior plays a pivotal role in workplace safety, although it is unlikely that either side will ever agree on whether it is more effective to prevent the unsafe behavior or to shield workers from the consequences of unsafe behaviors.

Worker injuries still represent a significant threat to workplace productivity and profitability. As long as billions of dollars continue to be wasted and lives lost, safety professionals will bitterly argue about the most effective way to attack the problem.

Why Behavior Based Safety Will Live Forever

Just when you think the debate over Behavior-Based Safety has faded from the landscape something brings it crashing back into your consciousness. For me, it was an article (and the response to it) by Dr. James Leemann. Jim asked the question "will Human and Organization Performance (HOP) finally supplant BBS" as the prevalent approach to worker safety? As one might suppose the BBS zealots and whack-jobs came crawling out of the woodwork to complain.

I'm a big proponent of HOP because it fixes system problems, not the blame. HOP goes beyond the behavior and addresses the system-wide antecedents, the things that precede and encourage the very behaviors that influence safety. I don't think it's a perfect system for protecting workers, but I believe that safety is the output of well-managed business systems and so HOP makes a lot of sense to my clients and me.

The backlash to Jim's article was predictable; the usual suspects accused Jim of not understanding BBS, not having seen BBS properly deployed, etc. etc. etc.

The whole argument exhausts me. I've said before that arguing against BBS is like telling someone that you don't like eating fricasseed squirrel anus. The first response is always, "well you just haven't had it cooked right; you need to try MY fricasseed squirrel anus—you'll love it!" So, you try their version and it tastes even worse than the last time.

But you still don't, in the eyes of the fricasseed squirrel anus lobby, have any real standing. How many squirrel anuses (anusi?) does a man have to eat before the nut jobs cooking it will allow that man to politely refuse on the grounds that squirrel anus is unpalatable?

To speak up against BBS is, in the mind fanatics, to speak out against safety, God, apple-pie and motherhood; it doesn't matter how much evidence you produce that BBS doesn't work, creates bloated bureaucracies, and encourages under-reporting of injuries, you will never convince the true believers that BBS is anything less than the one true path. It's like trying to convince Lynette "Squeaky" Fromme that Charles Manson isn't a pure soul; talking about it is like doing a card trick for a dog.

I'm at a loss to explain why BBS lingers in the same way I'm at a loss to explain why some people still believe in the Loch Ness Monster when most of the most credible evidence has since been exposed as so much bunk, or why there are Bigfoot sightings in every state of the Union (including Hawaii), or why people believe in alien autopsies while others refuse to believe that the moon landing was anything more than a government conspiracy with a Hollywood twist.

For some BBS is an important source of income and in those cases, it is not inconceivable that either they unethically cling to something that they know is snake oil or they have convinced themselves to ignore information that threatens their livelihoods; either way they have the strongest possible financial incentive to refute any claim that BBS doesn't work. It's much like a child who begins to doubt the existence of Santa Clause but is terrified that if he or she voices this doubt the Christmas gravy train will end and there will be no more Christmas present bonanza; the pragmatist in each of us will play it safe and perpetuate the Santa Claus myth even though long after we ourselves have long stopped believing.

For others, BBS is a crutch on which they lean to compensate for the lack of real competency in safety. When one doesn't quite get it, one clings to those things that they CAN understand. If you have a safety practitioner who lacks understanding of the basic safety regulations will find BBS a comforting alternative, with it's simplistic "just reward safe behaviors" philosophy. Many people who don't know the hard science side of safety will gravitate toward the simple argument that "if 80% of injuries are caused by behavior then we should focus on behaviors".

In a broader sense, BBS has a wide appeal to the key players within an organization. Management likes the "let's hold workers accountable for working safe" underpinnings of BBS. Safety professionals like the number of resources that fall under their control; they get to spend money and engage in a wide range of activities. Employees love the pizza parties and safety BINGOs and safety bonuses. And of course, vendors love the revenue it brings in. There is a conspiratorial feel to all this that sets off alarm bells.

Still others and I believe this is the largest group speak about BBS in philosophical terms. Those in this group will insist vendors have a behavior-based safety system in place as a condition of doing business; it's a nice thought but what then constitutes a "behavior-based safety" system? Is it enough that the safety system address unsafe behaviors? If so, this is fundamentally flawed unless the definition includes some context, and because all behavior exists within a context the definition would have to be exhaustive to be of any use whatever. What's that old saying about the road to Hell being paved with good intentions? Wikipedia (granted nobody's vision of a credible source), defines Behavior Based Safety as "the "application of science of behavior change to real-world problems" or "(its error not mine). A process that creates a safety partnership between management and employees that continually focuses people's attention and actions on theirs, and others, daily safety behavior. BBS (again their screw up) "focuses on what people do, analyzes why they do it, and then applies a research-supported intervention strategy to improve what people do" Let's take that one phrase at a time:

"application of science of behavior change" according to behaviorscience.com the science of behavior change is behaviorism. And according to the American Board of Professional Psychology (people who it would seem ought to know) "behaviorism" "emphasizes an experimental-clinical approach to the application of behavioral and cognitive sciences to understand human behavior and develop interventions that enhance the human condition." I'm pretty sure that BBS as practiced is just about as far from this as can be reasonably imagined.

"A process that creates a safety partnership between management and employees that continually focuses people's attention and actions on theirs, and others, daily safety behavior". Here, while many BBS systems aspire to this, none can honestly say they have achieved it, for if such a system does exist there would be no injuries, no near misses, no need for the hapless companies to frantically feed the BBS money machine.

"focuses on what people do, analyzes why they do it, and then applies a research-supported intervention strategy to improve what people do" Again, while BBS may do all these things, to what end? They haven't and never will prove that all this focus and research changes human behavior one whit, nor does it change the ingrained tendency for people to make errors, take risks, and behave unpredictably. No, I am not condemning anyone who requires his or her vendors to have a behavior-based safety system—just using safety performance as a criterion for selection will save more lives than not doing so—I am not condemning anything really, I just want to know why merely asking the question "is it time to dump BBS and consider another approach" is seen as abject ignorance or malicious heresy. Is a world without BBS so threatening and scary?

Four Flaws of Behavior-Based Safety

There is a growing body of evidence that BBS does more harm than good (the current head of the OSHA recently expressed his concerns that incentives and BBS were creating a climate where not reporting injuries is more important than preventing injuries. That is not to say that there are no studies on the wonderful effectiveness of BBS (although a fair amount funded by companies that make tens of millions of dollars selling it). So how can studies show diametrically opposed points of view?

For starters, there is no international standard that differentiates BBS from well... BS. Anyone can describe his or her particular flavor of snake oil as Behavior Based Safety. Read the admittedly less than universally respected reference Wikipedia article on BBS and it reads like a brochure written by the closed-head injured; it is far from impartial, and anyone who dares question the value of BBS is soundly shouted down. The vagueness with which people talk about BBS is astonishing (and no, I don't include everyone in this condemnation, but let's face it there are a lot of quacks out there selling some quasi-psychobabble as BBS and it has hurt anyone who labels his or her approach to worker safety as BBS.)

Here's a thought. What if we stopped creating labels for our safety? would it kill us if we didn't keep trotting out a new complex safety panacea? Behaviors cause injuries. I get it, but there is plenty more to consider (whether or not the behavior was the result of conscious, informed decision making, for starters) than individual behavior (like how individuals behave differently in a population, or the innate,

120

uncontrollable variation in human behavior to name two.)

Honestly there are so many people who are so quick to jump to defend BBS it really makes me suspicious of whether it is the methodology or their livelihoods that they are so adamant about protecting (again, Dominic, I am not throwing stones at you, but having just returned from a major safety conference where I heard dozens of specious arguments about why more people should invest in BBS that I could just pull my hair out.

And while we're at it, how many of the new charlatans selling culture change solutions where schilling half-baked BBS five years ago? Until I hear a BBS proponent that will even consider that there are other, perhaps better solutions out there, I will continue to be skeptical. Too many of these professionals are process zealots—they care far more about the methodology than the results, and that's dangerous. These people will always dismiss individual cases (whether it be an injury or a catastrophe) as statistical outliers or anomalies or in some way the fault of someone else.

If BBS is so clearly the best solution, why does it need defending? And why are there so many hotly contested variations of it? When was the last time people defended the concept of gravity with such visceral intensity?

I understand that several giants of BBS certify safety professionals in their methodologies. It's a great business model: safety professionals, buoyed by their newfound sense of importance and portable credentials, become advocates for your methodology. They will push and advocate your system and you will make money hand over fist. If you can live with the fact that people will not be protected while you make huge profits I guess this is a pretty good life.

More and more companies are finding Behavior-Based Safety Programs just don't deliver what they promise and are moving to a more balanced and practical approach to managing worker Health and Safety. Executives are drawn to Behavior-Based Safety Programs because they promise quick and painless results. Safety professionals are attracted to the idea that worker behavior is the cause of most workplace injuries. Unfortunately, experts are beginning to question whether or not Behavior-Based Safety is based on a foundation of flawed premises.

Flaw 1: Behavior is a contributor in 93 percent of injuries.

On the surface, this kind of statistic would certainly seem to argue strongly in favor of a Behavior-Based Safety Program, but it is a specious argument. 100 percent of injuries have a behavioral element. The formula for an injury is Hazard + Interaction + Catalyst = Injury. By definition, an interaction is behavioral in nature, so essentially the argument that unsafe behavior accounts for 93 percent of all injuries is akin to saying, "If workers didn't DO anything, they wouldn't get hurt." Fair statement, but then who wants a workplace where no work is done?

Flaw 2: Behavior modification is an effective tool in reducing workplace injuries.

Most Behavior-Based Safety Programs rely on recognition and rewards to positively reinforce safe behaviors and discourage unsafe behaviors. So, basically, a worker is forced to choose between seeking treatment and receiving a safety incentive. If you had told me when I was building seats for the General Motors Fleetwood Plant that I would get a $50 quarterly bonus if I didn't get injured, you would not hear about any of my injuries unless I left the plant in an ambulance. What tends to happen in these programs is that inflammation of the elbow turns into tendonitis which then turns into carpal tunnel syndrome and the resulting cost of treatment is astronomical. Research has shown that such systems are certainly effective at discouraging the reporting of injuries, but there is little evidence that behavior modification has any sustainable effect on the corporate culture. (Yes, ergonomics nerds I know it doesn't work that way, it's what we like to call a metaphor, now shut up and let the grown-ups talk.

Flaw 3: Unsafe behavior is deliberate.

Behavior-Based Safety starts with the premise that if workers were more careful, less of them would get hurt. This philosophy appeals to many executives who, frustrated by a lack of progress in reducing injuries, would like to put the burden for workplace safety back onto the worker. Two better premises are "nobody wants to get hurt" and "no system is designed to hurt workers." If these premises are true, no amount of behavior modification will lower worker injuries.

Flaw 4: People take unnecessary risks because they are careless.

In the many incident investigations that I have conducted where behavior played a key causative or proximate role, the clear majority of the injured workers took the risk because a) they were trying to show initiative and save time, and b) they were unaware of the magnitude of the risk they were taking, and/or c) they didn't believe the risk was credible. Very few of these injured workers believed they were putting themselves in serious jeopardy.

So, is Behavior-Based Safety so deeply flawed that there is no room for recognition programs in a world-class safety process? Absolutely not; here are some tips for integrating recognition programs into your safety process:

- Reward the Right Things. Instead of rewarding workers for not getting injured, reward them for identifying system flaws that cause injuries. A reward for a suggestion that makes the workplace safer is far more meaningful than one for "collective safety" where an entire department is rewarded for going without an injury.

- Understand and Correct the Root Causes of Unsafe Behaviors. It's not enough to identify unsafe behaviors; to truly improve workplace safety, one has to take proactive steps to remove hazards (both process flaws AND unsafe behaviors) before people get hurt. Rewarding workers who identify and correct the root causes of injuries is a good use of recognition and reward programs.

- Don't Jump to Conclusions About Behaviors. Use "repetitive whys" to understand the thought processes that lead to unsafe behaviors before reacting to them. More often than not, the process dictates the behavior.

What's Wrong With Drinking The Kool-Aid?

ISHN published an article by me (about the uselessness of slogans) that has drawn a fair amount of both criticisms and questions. In one case, a long-time reader and friend posted something of a response, and though I am arrogant, I am not arrogant enough to believe that his LinkedIn post was completely directed at me. I AM arrogant enough to believe that his post was at least somewhat prompted by the article. A few days later, I received a request to join the network of someone who too read the post/article and voiced her concern on how best to address the tendency on the part of both safety "professionals" (her quotes, not mine) and corporate leaders to push, slogan-based pseudo-psychological time and money wasting activities so pervasive in the safety field.

I believe that there is a great philosophical divide in safety that one can illustrate as a four-quadrant model. On one axis we have behaviour (I adopted the Anglo spelling of the word because that's the way most of the world spells it) on one end and process at the other; all safety practitioners fall somewhere along this continuum. The other axis is bordered by individual responsibility versus organizational responsibility. What this means is that everyone who derives a living from safety believes that either injuries are caused by behaviours or process flaws and either the organization or the individual bears primary responsibility for safety. For the record, I am a centrist in this debate although like most I can drift to a quadrant depending on my mood or the topic or even what I had for lunch.

As I have said on many occasions, I ardently believe that there are tools that simply don't belong in the safety toolbox. For example, there are still people out there that believe that disciplining workers for getting injured is a useful tool. While it is certainly appropriate to discipline people for recklessness, I don't believe that it is ever appropriate to discipline people for human error, that is, something they didn't intend to do and yet made an honest mistake. This is just one example of a "tool" that I think most people would agree doesn't belong in the safety toolbox. I am taking the easy way out, of course, but there are a fair many more controversial tools that I could have mentioned but that would simply raise the hackles of many safety professionals and would interfere with an unemotional debate.

I have posted that "it's just a tool and every tool in the toolbox has a use" is a tired argument and I believe that it is; it's what people say when they can't construct a logical argument against a point I make that questions the value of a "safety" activity. Saying "twisting the heads of ducks is just one tool in the safety professional's toolbox" is just a passive-aggressive way of saying "well that's YOUR opinion". And while we are all entitled to our opinions, we aren't all entitled to our own facts and truth. I may believe that Bigfoot built Buckingham Palace, but I can't shield my stupidity behind the adage "everyone is entitled to their own opinion." Yes, everyone has the right to be wrong. Say what you want about me, but there is nothing passive about my aggression. I make these points because I want to get to the heart of the issue, and that issue is the alarming frequency with which safety practitioners use superstition and folk wisdom instead of science. Nobody likes to be told that their cherished tools are useless gibberish but at some point, we have to call the emperor naked.

Too often we in safety start with a solution and work backward to make it fit the problem; we begin using the tools and methods that we enjoy, find easy to use, or that we understand. It's human nature to gravitate to the familiar and safety practitioners are no different. I've called techniques psychobabble and antiquated. Some of these "tools" flat-out don't work and others may still work, but there are far better, more effective and less expensive ways of accomplishing the same thing. I include Behaviour Based Safety as one of these tools. As many of you know, I am an outspoken critic of BBS. Why? because if you ask 10 BBS proponents to define it you are likely to get 11 different responses.

How can a methodology be effective when its top proponents and advocates can't seem to agree on its very definition? I honestly believe that it does lead to a "blame-the-worker" mentality. Not in all cases of course, but the danger is real and always there. When I make these criticisms, people don't defend BBS they say I don't understand it or that the organizations that I have seen have implemented it inappropriately. We can blame the organization as improperly applying the methods or tools, and we can blame the BBS practitioner as being misguided, or we can blame a host of other things, but the damage is still done.

For the record, I don't believe that everyone who sells or advocates BBS is selling snake oil or a knuckle-dragger, but some are. Many believe that what they are doing is the best bet for improving worker safety, others have spent their career selling something that is increasingly dubious and when it comes to safety this is unconscionable. But as my LinkedIn colleague pointed out, clouding the water by filling the C+ suite's heads with ill-defined schemes for making the workplace safer puts workers at risk.

Many BBS practitioners advocate behaviour modification as a useful tool for "changing our lives for the better" and I couldn't agree more. But shy of a cult, behaviour modification is typically not successful in changing the behaviour of a population. The workplace is an interactive population and the sciences of sociology, anthropology, and other social sciences are ignored by many BBS theorists. Frankly were it possible to use behaviour modification to change the behaviours of a population we could end war, crime and a host of societal issues by using it. We would live in a Utopian society…and yet we don't.

When I post it is my ardent hope that safety professionals will rethink their practices and ask themselves if what they are doing is returning value that is commensurate with the cost and effort that it requires. Alas, far too many in the safety community are unwilling to even consider change and will always keep tools in their toolbox solely because they like them and are comfortable using them even if they are destructive and dangerous.

How do we make these safety practitioners understand that their ideas are misguided, nonscientific, and dangerous? Sadly, I don't have any answers. How do you convince Jenny McCarthy that her contention that vaccinations cause autism is not based in science and that using her celebrity to raise awareness of hokum is recklessly endangering children? People can argue that her position is dangerously wrong, but their arguments fall on deaf ears. How do you use logic to sway people from a persistent emotional belief? You don't. Now, imagine these people who are so emotionally tied to an erroneous belief derive their incomes by getting others to invest in these emotional beliefs. You don't have another tool in the toolbox you have another glassy-eyed convert lining up for a glass of Kool-Aid. And what's wrong with someone "drinking the Kool-Aid"? Let us never forget that the expression "drinking the Kool-Aid" refers to the mass murder-suicide of the members of Jim Jones' People's Temple followers. So, what's wrong with "drinking the Kool-Aid"? It's laced with cyanide.

CHAPTER 6

When the Pen Drips Poison

Everyone Is An Idiot Except Me

Somewhere, perhaps over a beer, a safety professional is bemoaning the lack of a safety culture at his or her employer. Said safety professional protests loudly that, quoting Butch Cassidy And the Sundance Kid "I have vision and the whole world is wearing bifocals." He or she raises his voice in frustration and righteous indignation that he or she has it all figured out, that it's easy in fact, but for the idiots in the workplace who can't seem to help how stupid they are; they don't follow the rules, take stupid risks, and well…generally, act like idiots. They don't have common sense, in fact, they don't have the sense that God gave geese. No brains at all.

And these self-righteous safety professionals shake their heads in disgusted disbelief at the difficulty they have in shielding the dolts they are charged with protecting from the logical consequences of their own stupidity. They can see the Promised Land but can't seem to sell it to the great unwashed. If only people would follow their sterling examples, and take safety more seriously.

Safety professionals are the Rodney Dangerfields of the workplace—they get no respect no matter how hard they try. I've been taken to task by a lot of you recently. I've been accused of deliberately provoking safety professionals by insulting their most cherished institutions. One perky safety hero even accused me of being unethical, although despite his pithy criticisms seemed incapable of citing anything that I might have done that was even remotely questionable. Clearly, I have offended many of the true believers and the risk of doing so again, let's talk about the whacky safety photos that wriggle through the email boxes of safety professionals like drunken eels. I'd estimate that about 75% of safety professionals have used actual photos of extremely dangerous and reckless acts in some form of safety training or communication. Far more distribute these emails and yuck it up around the water cooler. Out of one side of their pie holes, they cluck their tongues about workers that don't take things seriously while circulating photos of electricians working on wiring while standing on an aluminum ladder in a swimming pool. Would these safety professionals think this was so hysterical if they learned that the worker was electrocuted immediately after the photo was taken? If safety professionals can't look at these photos as something alarming, as something indicative of the state of safety in developing nations, then how can they expect laypeople to do so? And before some self-righteous mouth breather hammers out an angergram and asks if I have used these photos, yes I have; I used these photos to demonstrate how little regard people have for safety. I have used them to demonstrate how people are driven to expediency and will often be blind to very serious hazards. Seen in the right light these photos can be powerful "coachable moments" and of course I am not criticizing those of you who use them in this regard (you wouldn't believe how many indignant emails I get from safety professionals who defend the stupidity of the field by telling me all about how they aren't guilty of what I am describing. Honestly, who gives a steaming pile of dung? What drives people to defend someone else's asinine practices by offering a less heinous act as proof that not all people who behave badly are evil? But then I digress.)

Consider this, someone decided to snap a photo of people in imminent danger of being killed INSTEAD of intervening. The photographer knew the situation was remarkably dangerous but chose to photograph it instead of containing the risk, coaching the people exposed to the dangers, and correcting the hazard. Many Just Culture advocates are quick to remind us that we don't have a legal obligation to save a life. Some might argue that we don't have a moral obligation to save a life (I would argue the opposite, but ultimately the answer to that is between the one who asks and his or her maker,) But the sheer cold-blooded nature of taking a photo of a life-threatening situation when one could do something to stop it is troubling. And circulating the photos is the same moral turpitude as circulating snuff films or pornography—these things cease to exist without consumers. Unless people promote these photos maybe people will stop taking them and start intervening. Of course, the average person is probably blithely ignorant of the larger social context, but safety professionals cannot claim such immunity.

The hypocrisy doesn't end with, let's face it, essentially harmless photos circulated by some innocuous safety guys. Ladies and gentlemen, I submit exhibit B: the Darwin Awards. Named for noted hypochondriac and intrepid naturalist explorer, Charles Darwin, the Darwin Awards celebrate people who improve the gene pool by dying while doing something spectacularly stupid circumstances. I've never met a safety professional who hasn't heard of the Darwin Awards and most relate the more outlandish stories with drooling glee. But the Darwin Award is the pinnacle of blame-the-victim-thinking. Safety professionals who propagate the Darwin Awards by circulating links to the website should be ashamed.

Okay, enough of my self-righteous crap.

We all have a tendency to laugh at tragedy and we all have a tendency to have a double standard when it comes to risk. If I take a potentially life-threatening risk, I'm adventurous. If you take that same risk you're an idiot; a reckless clod who would be doing humanity a favor were you to die in a hilarious mishap. It's human nature. To err is human; to judge others for their errors is even more human. We will continue to feel superior to people who take truly stupid risks even while we photograph them while driving by and text pithy comments at 60 mph. I guess what gets me is the hypocrisy if this post is like most of my others it will generate some truly ugly email. That's okay, I'm thick-skinned and egotistical enough to take it.

Maybe I need to lighten up. Maybe it's okay to blame the victim. Maybe, as so many claim, these light-hearted looks at safety are harmless and I am just another bleeding heart who overreacts to what most people would characterize as good fun. Maybe. But maybe if the safety professionals didn't talk out of both sides of their mouths and send mixed signals to the workforce people would take them more seriously and just maybe they might create an environment where safety could become a valued part of the culture. Maybe.

Don't Read This Section...Navigating Through the Sea of Liars and Idiots

93% of information posted on the internet is wrong. Does that figure surprise you? Does it seem high? I made that up. I covered the American Society of Safety Engineers in Chicago on press for Facility Safety Management magazine. ASSE and the National Safety Council together drive more press coverage of worker safety than nearly everything else— not counting industrial disasters—combined.

Given that I had covered the show, I thought I would devote this section to an exploration of how we as safety professionals get our information and the efficacy of those sources.

Blogs
A weblog (or "Blog" as some apparently dyslexic mouth breather contracted it) is an uncontrolled outlet for the incoherent blathering of someone motivated enough to write on a topic but often not talented enough to be published. Blogs vary greatly from the pre-teen who rants about her English teacher to respected experts and authors who use blogging to round out their literary or journalistic retinue and everywhere in between. Because blogs are typically free, easy to create, and unrestricted the information is often rough and frequently dubious. Because this information is typically the work of one person and does not pass through a gatekeeper who vets work, editing the pieces that make the cut and rejecting those that don't (this process is referred to as a peer review). Blogs are not considered peer-reviewed and therefore researchers and other authors can't cite the work as a source of truth.

This discipline doesn't extend to us bloggers...we can create, promote, and perpetuate ignorance on an unprecedented scale. The misinformation many bloggers spew ranges from insipid (and usually incorrect) trivia to the truly dangerous lies and fear mongering. At their best blogs, are the highest and purest form of the freedom of speech but at their worst blogs are irresponsible propagation of specious arguments and urban legends.

Forums

Forums are online discussions moderated (hopefully) by a small group of devoted volunteers who enforce civility, discussion topics, and generally keep the group in line. Except for Penthouse Forum, forums are not considered peer-reviewed works and therefore cannot be cited as a source for academic works or research. Why? because forums are essentially just opinions that people support or refute. No third party does any fact-checking and the bulk of the discussion may not be supported by facts.

Newsletters

Newsletters are regular publications put out by non-journalistic organizations. Newsletters (despite being positioned otherwise) are marketing tools. A newsletter is at its heart a tool for marketing something. (Some of you may be ready to scream because you edit a "newsletter" for your professional organization or Not for Profit and you're not selling anything. I would challenge you that you are indeed selling something—like, for example, your organization's reputation. Because of the promotional nature of newsletters (and just because a publication is called a newsletter on the masthead doesn't make it a newsletter any more than The Wall Street Journal is an academic or scientific journal) they typically are not considered peer-reviewed publications even if they follow the same general vetting and editing process.

Magazines

Magazines are peer-reviewed publications. Most have highly competitive publishing criteria, a vetting process, a strong system of editing and fact-checking. Essentially this process produces a written piece that—while credited to a single author—is the work of a team of publishing professionals. This fairly intricate system of checks and balances, magazines are considered credible sources of truth and can be cited as sources in other works.

Journals and Periodicals

Journals and periodicals typically are compendiums of research findings from individual authors or writing teams. In many cases, these papers are presented at professional conferences and symposiums. The competition and acceptance criteria for these works are often fierce and rigorous, with authors submitting abstracts to a team that rejects most of the proposed abstracts. Those few that are accepted must produce a paper that is supported by research and cited sources. The paper is then again reviewed by the selection committee, which will often reject the initial draft and will continuing recommending edits until it is satisfied with the final result. At this point, the authors are typically invited to present the paper to an audience of his or her colleagues. This process can be exceedingly long and onerous. I wrote the paper Creating Safety in Offshore Operations for Loss Prevention 2010 and was invited to present my paper in Bruges, Belgium. The review and vetting process took almost 3 years. Sadly, I was unable to accept the invitation to speak owing to other commitments (it's tough to plan the disruption associated with an international symposium three years in advance on a maybe.)

In Europe and in U.S. academic circles it is not uncommon to expect the speakers to pay to attend the conference at which they are presenting. In short, very few proposed journal articles ever make it to publication in a journal and those that do represent the crème de la crème and are the closest thing we are likely to see as a source of truth on a given topic.

So, if blogs are so bad why do I write, not one, but two? I like to fine-tune my writing and flesh out ideas that I generally get arguing with idiots in forums. Those of you who regularly read my blogs, share groups with me on LinkedIn and read my published work may have noticed a progression in my work.   Typically, I get an idea by participating in a LinkedIn discussion or answering a question in the LinkedIn section devoted to that. From there I generally get enough of an idea (typically a response to someone who only wants to shout me down) to flesh out into a blog post. My blog posts tend to be longer than the publications for which I write will publish so I have to pare them down to a more manageable size—typically 1,000 words or less. From there I submit the article to an editor who cleans up the piece, renames it, puts art next to it, and streamlines it. I'd like to think that I work well in all these media but that is ultimately for you, the reader to judge.

Safety Slogans Don't Save Lives

Deming Was right—don't waste your time on them

It's tough to bring professionalism to a trade that actively looks to make itself look stupid. There are only so many hours in the day, only so many resources, and if we waste either it's tough to go to the well and ask for help and money.

And let's face it, as safety professionals we are perpetual victims, unloved, overworked, and most of all understaffed and under-funded. On the other hand, we spend our scarce time and meager resources doing things that don't reduce the risk of injuries, reduce our operating costs or do really much of anything.

Chief among the waste-of-time activities that make us look out of touch with any semblance of reality is the creation and promotion of safety slogans. What is the purpose of safety slogans? Deming specifically signaled out slogans in his tenth point for management, "Eliminate slogans, exhortations, and targets for the workforce asking for zero defects and new levels of productivity. Such exhortations only create adversarial relationships, as the bulk of the causes of low quality and low productivity belongs to the system and thus lies beyond the power of the workforce."

Creating adversaries

Do safety slogans create adversarial relationships? In a way they do. The fact that we post safety slogans implies that were it not for our little gems of wisdom, the great unwashed would stick their entire heads in the machinery. At their worst, safety slogans patronize and demean the worker.

Am I stating things too strongly? I don't think so. Safety slogans don't raise awareness of safety; it raises and reinforces the awareness that safety professionals think themselves superior to the people who turn wrenches for a living. It widens the gulf between blue and white color. And while safety professionals may not recognize Deming for his genius, I think he hit the nail on the head with this point. If we believe that all but the rarest injuries are the result of either unintended actions (human error/accidents) or poorly calculated risks, then a pithy saying isn't likely to have much of an effect.

Who among you has ever read a safety slogan and thought, "Wow, I've been approaching my life completely wrong. I'm completely turned around on this. I need to make some changes."

The long and the short of it is safety slogans serve no purpose, offer no benefit, and yet we devote precious time and money to thinking them up, launching campaigns around them, and promoting them as if they were a crucial part of our efforts to lower risks. So why do we persist in engaging in an activity that does nothing but make us look ridiculous in the eyes of the organization? And make no mistake, thinking up safety slogans doesn't garner safety professionals the respect or esteem of the organization because they coined the phrase, "Safety: It's Better Than Dying."

Don't curry favor

We do it because we like it, and we never ask the question, "Is this activity in the furtherance of safety?" Sometimes misguided executives press us to come up with a slogan and eager to curry favor, we rush forward in an orgy of sycophantic fervor delighted at the exposure to the C-suite. Trust me when I tell you this is exposure you can do without.

As uncomfortable as it may be, we are better served by declining this request and fetching coffee and bagels instead. We don't need exposure that perpetuates the C-suite view of safety as simpletons who you call when you want something a kindergarten teacher would refuse to do. Far better to explain to the executive that your finite time would be better spent engaging in an activity that would return real business results.

Doing "fun" completely wrong

Not many safety professionals feel comfortable speaking up to an executive, but your first interactions with executives set a tone for the relationship. Do you want to be taken seriously? It begins here. When I have railed against safety slogans before, I invariably get some soft-baked safety guy roll his eyes, smirk and ask, "What's wrong with having a little fun with safety?" I am something of an expert in fun (I have had fun that will forever keep me out of any elected office, has gotten me barred from entire countries, and damn near got me killed on multiple occasions), and I am here to tell you that if you think that coming up with safety slogans is fun, you are out of your mind. You are doing "fun" completely wrong. I wouldn't even categorize thinking up safety slogans as amusing or as a brief respite from mind-crushing boredom. Let me be clear: I think safety slogans are stupid and make us look like simpletons. Deming was right, we have got to get rid of them.

CHAPTER 7

SAFETY AROUND THE WORLD

Asleep on the Job: The lethal connection between falls from height and sleep deprivation

Working at heights remains one of the most intrinsically dangerous industrial activities. A fall from heights means, if not certain death, a serious and perhaps crippling injury. Yet despite this, many organizations still face a tough time getting workers to use fall protection.

Background

According to the UK's Health and Safety Executive (HSE), two thirds of fatal injuries to workers are caused by only four kinds of injuries – one of which is falls from height. Falls, slips and trips combined made up more than half of all reported major injuries, and almost a third of injuries lasting more than three days.

Experts agree that the best way to protect against injuries caused by falling from heights is to avoid working at height in the first place, but it is seldom that simple. In many parts of the world, working at height is a one of the most common occupational requirements. This is particularly prevalent in the construction sector, but working at height injuries are also common in agriculture, oil and gas and even service industries.

According to the HSE, an average of 50 people die in Great Britain annually because of falls from height. In 2012 the HSE reported that 26% of all fatal construction site accidents were caused by falls from height. What's more, although injuries caused by falls from height represent only 13% of the overall injuries, a staggering 53% of fatalities were caused by falls from height.

Compliance issues

While very little research has been conducted to determine the exact cause of these falls it is fairly certain that most, if not all of these injuries could have been prevented had the workers properly used fall protection. As with all personal protective equipment (PPE), the most common failure is a lack of worker compliance.

Given the dangers faced when working at heights, a lack of compliance seems insane. After all, what possible reason could a worker have for taking such a reckless risk? Often workers decide that fall protection is unnecessary because they believe that falling from heights is a problem limited to the construction industry, or because they don't consider the height at which they will be working high enough to cause injury.

According to the QBE Insurance Issues Forum, however, 59% of major injuries occur following a fall from height of less than two metres, and 61% of more than three day injuries occur within the service industry.

Sleep deprivation

Before you blame the worker, or even the PPE itself for workplace incidents, consider that the worker may be sleep deprived. Often, when a worker is confronted for violating the policy requiring fall protection, he or she will likely shrug and say, "I forgot." Forgetting to wear gear that is so much a part of the work routine may sound like a lame excuse, but it may not be. Many safety professionals are realising that human errors, behavioural drift and even recklessness can be traced to a growing threat to workplace safety –a lack of sleep.

Many of us worry about not getting enough sleep, but just how harmful is a lack of sleep? As detailed in the following points, the short answer is – very.

A lack of sleep is as dangerous as alcoholic impairment. Experts contend that when someone has been awake for 21 hours, he/she will perform at a level of impairment roughly the same as a person with a blood alcohol level of 0.08%. Obviously, companies would never condone a worker who is under the influence of alcohol working at heights, yet these same organisations often knowingly allow sleep deprived employees to work in this condition.

Just like alcohol or drug use, a lack of sleep increases risky behaviour. Dr Chan's 2012 research found that a workplace incident is four times more likely to be caused by fatigue then buy alcohol or drug impairment.

As outlined in the following sections, this impairment may endanger workers in several ways.

Impeded judgment

Sleep deprivation impedes the worker's judgment, and it may cause an otherwise compliant worker to choose not to wear fall protection equipment. A sleep deprived worker is also far more likely to misjudge the height at which he/she is working, causing the previously mentioned reasoning that fall protection equipment is not necessary.

Lack of manual dexterity

A sleep impaired worker is far more likely to struggle to wear the fall protection equipment properly. While most fall protection is easy to put on and properly fasten, the loss of manual dexterity typically associated with sleep deprivation may make improperly installed protection more common. The lack of manual dexterity coupled with slowed reactions may also prevent workers from acting in time to prevent a fall.

Lack of alertness

The drowsiness associated with sleep deprivation can jeopardise the safety when working at height in two ways: firstly, a sleep deprived worker is more likely to miss damage or other flaws in the pre-use inspection of the PPE, and secondly, this lack of alertness increases the probability that a fall will occur. The combined effect is a worker potentially using damaged PPE precisely when protection is needed the most.

Increased injuries

Even if we were to design completely foolproof fall protection equipment, sleep deprivation threatens workers in ways that PPE can't protect against. According to a 2010 study by the University of British Columbia, Canadians who worked night and rotating shifts were almost twice as likely to be injured on the job when compared with those working regular day shifts.

Multiple sources list fatigue as one of the top five causal factors in workplace incidents (Chan, 2010), so while experts may attribute upward of 90% of workplace injuries to unsafe behaviour, most fail to answer the question of why a worker behaved unsafely. Increasingly, that answer is linked to a lack of sleep.

A fatigued worker is far more likely to miss critical steps in a process, such as ensuring they are wearing appropriate fall protection, keeping the fall protection equipment in good working condition, and choosing the right locations to which they tie off.

Vegso et al (2007) found an 88% increased risk of an incidents for individuals working more than 64 hours a week. As employers try to do more work with fewer workers, workers are often forced to work while sleep deprived. As workers tire they make more mistakes and riskier choices.

Extent of the threat

So, just how widespread is the threat? Considering that almost a third of us don't get enough sleep, the problem is at epidemic proportions. In 2012, the US Centers for Disease Control and Prevention reported that 50 to 70 million American adults suffer from sleep and wakefulness disorders.

Similar studies in the UK not only found that many people suffer from a lack of sleep, but also that sleep deprivation can interfere with people's ability to perform demanding cognitive tasks. When a worker is at height, decisions relative to tying off, for example, could be undermined to the extent that the worker effectively has no protection from falls whatsoever.

Little sleep, lower compliance

UK studies also found that too little sleep caused an increase in irritability. This increase in irritability makes it more likely that workers will deliberately violate rules that they find objectionable, refuse to wear fall protection equipment that they feel is unwarranted or that they dislike because it is uncomfortable – or just to be plain obstinate.

The UK studies also found that a lack of sleep caused perceptual disturbances – a difficulty seeing or hearing, for example. These perceptual disturbances can easily cause a worker to justify violating fall protection requirements because they have erroneously judged the height at which they will be working as safer than it actually is.

Poor decision making

According to Hallinan, even moderate sleep deprivation can cause brain impairment equivalent to driving while drunk – and has been shown to significantly increase an individual's willingness to take risks.

In effect, sleep deprived workers make more mistakes, poorer decisions, and take more risks – all things that have been repeatedly shown to increase the probability of worker injuries.

British researchers reached a similar conclusion and in one study found that "Sleep loss has a primary effect on Sleepiness and Sustained Attention with much smaller effects on challenging Working Memory tasks." In simpler terms, the research found that workers are far more likely to forget rote tasks – like wearing PPE – when they were deprived of sleep on a regular basis.

Lack of sleep makes us sick

According to USNews.com lack of sleep has been tied to mental distress, depression, anxiety, obesity, hypertension, diabetes, high cholesterol and certain risk behaviours including cigarette smoking, physical inactivity and heavy drinking.

The National Sleep Foundation found that after seven days of too little sleep the body undergoes genetic changes to as many as 700 genes. What's more, researchers still don't understand exactly the implications of these genetic changes. Clearly, sleep deprivation is far more dangerous than many people realise.

Despite the dangers, there are very few legal requirements that govern the lack of sleep for most workers and of those trades typically governed – healthcare workers, airline pilots, and truck drivers, for example – the workers aren't the most likely to die from a fall from height.

In fact, in most municipalities, the legal duties incumbent on organisations are fairly vague and most fall in one of the following categories (where it is reasonably practicable):

- Avoid working at heights • Prevention of falls • Minimise the consequence of the fall

While working at heights regulations require those insured to ensure that their health and safety management systems:

- Enable them to plan all work at height
- Apply the hierarchy of control measures
- Select the right people and equipment for the task •

- Train persons doing the work •
- Inspect and maintain equipment used
- Ensure supervision and monitoring of work as per the plans set out

There are no specific requirements that those working at heights be fit for duty. The closest thing there is to such a requirement is the provision "work at height must be 'carried out in a manner which is so far as is reasonably practicable safe'."

Obviously, work performed at heights by a sleep deprived worker is not being carried out in a manner that is safe, but is it reasonably practicable to expect organisations to manage sleep deprivation?

Recognising the signs

Managing the sleep deprived can be challenging, but considering that the impairment can be as significant as that of alcohol use it's important not only for the safety of the sleep deprived, but other workers as well.

When it comes to sleep deprived employees there really isn't a meaningful distinction from other signs of unfitness for duty:

- Sudden changes in appearance. The sleep deprived employee may seem to lose interest in their appearance. A normally neat and appropriately dressed worker who suddenly reports to work dishevelled may be unfit for duty. Managers have a right and responsibility to assertively confront the worker and have a frank conversation about the worker's fitness to work]

- Increased mistake making. A worker who has otherwise shown competency at his or her job who then becomes prone to errors may be showing signs of sleep deprivation.

Managers should investigate the causes of this sudden drop in performance.

- Increased lapses in judgment. Just as the sleep deprived worker will make more mistakes, a worker with normally

146

sound judgment will show more incidences of poor choices and bad decision making

- Irritability. A lack of sleep will make a usually good natured worker ill-tempered and irritable. Many workers who are branded as having a bad attitude may simply not be getting enough sleep

Willing but unable

Sleep deprivation in the workplace shows no signs of abating, but there's still hope.

Organisations should educate workers in ways that they can get enough restful sleep.

Experts at the National Sleep Foundation and elsewhere are resources in this effort and offer tips for getting a good night's sleep:

1. Don't sleep in at weekends – maintain your weekday sleep schedules.

2. Wind down. Experts recommend that people establish a regular relaxing routine to transition between waking and sleep. Soaking in a hot tub and then reading a book before retiring can greatly improve the quality of sleep one gets. Make your bedroom sleep friendly – dark, quiet, comfortable and cool.

3. Use your bed for sleeping. Experts warn that watching television or working on a computer can impede your ability to truly relax when it comes time for sleeping.

4. Avoid caffeine, nicotine and alcohol for several hours before bedtime.

5. Allow enough to time for sleep. Before you raise your hands in protest that you would if you could, consider that people who get enough sleep are significantly more productive than those who are deprived.

6. Nap. A 20 minute (no more) nap followed by exercise will make

you feel refreshed and provide you a pick-me-up that will make you more productive.

7. Finish eating at least two to three hours before your regular bedtime.

8. Exercise regularly and complete your workout a few hours before bedtime.

Recognise that one of the most common reasons for insomnia is worrying about not getting enough sleep. Lying quietly with one's eyes closed can be very restorative, and while it is not as healthy as deep REM sleep, it can be a short term solution to the sleep deprivation problem.

Dr. Charles Samuels, the medical director at the Centre for Sleep and Human Performance in Calgary, Alberta, offers some additional tips for avoiding sleep deprivation and fatigue:

1. Determine how much sleep you need to feel well rested on a daily basis. Multiply that number by seven. The resulting number is the amount of sleep you need per week.

2. Determine how much sleep you get. Add up the total amount of sleep you get on day/afternoon/evening shifts per week and night shift per week. Then determine your sleep debt in each situation by subtracting those numbers from your sleep need.

3. Focus on minimising your total sleep debt by taking the following actions:

    Improve your day sleep environment
    Catch up on your sleep on your days off
    Learn to catnap
    Sleep longer during the day when you have a night rotation or tour of duty
    Give yourself a quiet, completely dark, comfortable day sleep environment with no distractions.
    Try to get two three to four hour blocks of sleep during the day when you work the night shift.
    Learn to catnap. Take a short 20-30 minutes of time with eyes closed, situated in a comfortable resting position. You do not have to sleep to get

the benefit of a catnap.

Remember – the treatment for sleepiness and fatigue is SLEEP!

Safety professionals should raise the awareness of this problem among workers and share these tips for getting enough sleep, especially on the night shift. But if workers ignore these suggestions and continue to deprive themselves of sleep to the extent that they become a danger to their safety and the safety of others, the supervisors have no choice but to intervene. As ridiculous as it may seem, workers may need to be disciplined for not getting enough sleep.

There is no way of definitively knowing the full connection between sleep deprivation and falls from heights. It would, however, be foolish to discount the impact the profound effects can have even from short term sleep deprivation. Someone working at height should have no impairment to manual dexterity, judgment, or the ability to verify one's correct usage of the protective equipment – much less be more prone to risk taking.

5 Steps To Becoming A More Successful Safety Leader

Successful

safety

> As OHS professionals advance through their careers, they need to become less of an auditor with an encyclopedic knowledge of safety regulations, and more of a businessperson.

If you love your job but find yourself ambitious and upwardly mobile, you may be on a collision course with reality. As you advance in your career, so too do your day-to-day responsibilities. In my experience, the bigger the pay envelope, the bigger the headaches. So what does the safety leader need to learn to be successful?

1) Less preaching, more teaching. Nobody likes to listen to some sanctimonious gasbag lecture him or her on, well... anything, but particularly safety and the right thing to do. Most business schools don't teach a class on safety, and so most executives have learnt what they know about safety from the safety people with whom they've worked over the years. It is your role to teach them that no enterprise can be truly successful if it continues to hurt workers. As long as safety professionals don't have the right to fire you (with no hope of appeals to leadership or the Union), safety professionals are fairly impotent when it comes to swinging the hammer. I was recently working as a production safety consultant (a job held in such little esteem that it doesn't appear in the credits, although the catering company does) when one of the crew, a tall and burly brute, would always make it a point to make a snide comment about "the safety guy". "Okay, everybody better watch out, the safety guy is here", he would say in exaggerated fear and awe whenever he saw me approach. "Everybody better make sure you're following all the rules." It was irritating. In fact, it bugged the living crap out of me. I was there to do a job; nothing more, nothing less. I wasn't looking for reasons to jam anybody up, in fact, that was the last thing I wanted. Like everyone else on this very dangerous movie set, I just wanted to do my job and go home under my own power in my own car instead of an ambulance or a coroner's wagon. (Those who don't work in safety seem to forget that safety professionals are often put in the most dangerous situations on a given site. I've walked across catwalks that were corroded so badly that I could feel them start to give, which would have sent me tumbling 14 stories to the concrete below; I've had poisonous gas vented just below me; worked in a mine where the entire camp's soil was flammable; and been nearly struck by countless recklessly driven vehicles.) My goal, selfishly, is to go home safe every day, and if I can do it while helping others to go home safe as well, so much the better. So one day I approached a group of crew building a set. We exchanged pleasantries and I asked them what they will be doing that day and what, if any, safety concerns they might have. It was fairly routine work and these guys were experts, so I just left them with a "I'll check in with you later just to see if you need anything, but if anything comes up just hit me on the radio", and walked away. As I was leaving, my old buddy the town crier came up to me with a sneer and in a challenging voice filled with disdain asked, "So, Mr Safety, is everyone following the rules?" I looked at him and said, "Look, I don't know who you think I am so let me make something clear. I'm not your mother and I'm not your boss. My job isn't to get you to follow the rules, I can't fire you, I can't write you up, in fact, there's nothing I can do to force you to follow the rules. I'm here to help you to make informed decisions about the safety of the choices you make. So I would appreciate it if you stopped treating me like I'm your babysitter or your substitute teacher. I give advice; you can take it and maybe it will save your life or keep you from killing someone, or you can ignore it and kill yourself or someone else. The choice is entirely up to you." From that point on he never announced my visit except to say, "Good morning, Phil". He was friendly and congenial and I grew to like him very much. Going into this situation I had absolutely no authority or power, and this is the same for most people reading this – whether you are a safety neophyte fresh from university or a grizzled veteran with 30 plus years on the job. What's more, as you advance through your career you need to become less of an auditor with an encyclopedic knowledge of safety regulations and more of a businessperson.

2) Know the cost of injuries. Forget multipliers and industry averages, they aren't real to most operations leaders, but "those aren't our numbers" calculate the direct (and as much as possible, indirect) cost of every injury. It may take some doing – these costs are all recorded but they tend to be scattered across the organisation. Safety leaders need to have these costs be more than a number, however. When an operations leader asks how that number was calculated or what that number means, the safety leader must be prepared with a quick and easily understood answer. Many people find it difficult to calculate the cost of injuries. The table on the following page illustrates the relative ease of applying real, known costs to injuries.

"My goal, selfishly, is to go home safe every day, and if I can do it while helping others to go home safe as well, so much the better"

Cost for each of these categories is calculated by multiplying the worker's wage with the amount of time it took to perform a task; for example, if it takes 10 minutes (there and back) to escort a worker to the clinic or plant nurse, and the escort makes $10.00, that time cost the company $100. The difficult thing about calculating the cost of the injury is getting an accurate time. When I have worked with clients, I have rewritten their incident investigation form to include the time for these tasks (which includes filling out the paperwork). Most of my clients are shocked at how big and real an impact a single injury can have on the company's bottom line, and all this is aside from the human cost, which as we all know can be tremendous and life-changing. Once you know the cost of an injury you can reduce these costs even if you don't eliminate the injury, which is a good indicator of severity, but also something as simple as the time it takes to complete the witness interviews (the sooner you conduct the interviews the faster they tend to go as people are still fresh and engaged and not struggling to remember exactly what happened).

Calculation of the cost of injuries

Cost of incident response	Wages	Time	Cost	Activity	Time	Cost
Injured worker wage	$ 14.00		$	Escort to medical		$
Medical wage	$ 37.00		$	Transport to clinic		$
Escort wage	$ 14.00		$	Spent at clinic 1		$
Safety wage $ $	$ 44.00		$	To enter on 300 log		$
Supervisor wage	$ 15.00		$	Supervisor intervention		$
Replacement worker wage	$ 14.00		$	Return from clinic		$
Est. cost of medical treatment of injuries	$			$		

Cost for non-recordable injuries	Wages	Time	Cost	Activity	Time	Cost
Medical wage	$ 37.00		$			
Safety wage	$ 44.00		$			
Supervisor wage	$ 15.00		$			
Medical Staff wage	$ 14.00		$			
Cost for Incident investigation						
Medical wage	$ 37.00		$			
Safety wage	$ 44.00		$			
Supervisor wage	$ 15.00		$			
Medical Staff wage	$ 14.00		$			

3) Influence, don't demand. The safety leader of the future has to be an astute politician, someone who can convince other function leaders of the business's justification for safety. Safety is more than just saving lives, it's about saving money. Injuries cost a lot of money, and successful safety leaders have to come down off their moral high horses ("safety is the right thing to do") and remember that the primary goal of every business is to stay in business, and to achieve this goal the business needs to make money. For many decades safety has been seen as a cost centre, not just by operations but by the safety professionals themselves. The safety leader must understand that every dollar spent on safety needs to enable safety, not impede it. A friend once said to me, "People nag when they have no power", and I think that is somewhat correct. Too many safety professionals nag the organisation in the name of influencing it. If your argument doesn't persuade me the first time you say it, saying it again over and over isn't likely to do anything but get my rancour up – I heard you the first time! Influence is the art of convincing me that what I want is what you want. It's the classic win-win scenario. It can be tough to convince someone that protecting workers is in a leader's best interests, and that is why money is such a good means of persuasion. In a very real sense, we are paid to do one of two things: we either make money for the company (which, by the way, scarce few of us do) or we are paid to save the company money (either through reducing waste or protecting the company from fines). Position your function in safety as a means of reducing waste (real waste that can be quantified and measured and make them look good) instead of merely protecting them from something that may or may not happen. Another good way of influencing is to get in the business of saying yes. Instead of shutting down an operation and lecturing a supervisor or worker about the importance of safety, suggest a safer way of doing things. Don't come at the person like an avenging angel full of recrimination, rather, approach as a trusted adviser who wants the same thing as the worker – to go home in one piece.

4) Speak the language of operations. I am surprised at the number of safety professionals, even safety leaders, who don't know their company's business model. Are you a sales organisation? Is production king? You must know the business model (in most basic terms, how your company makes money). I have seen safety professionals waste their careers fighting against the organisation's business model. "Leadership doesn't support me", they whine, when in truth they aren't supporting leadership. Safety leaders must understand the primary driver of the organisation and express injury costs in those terms. If your company has a sales culture, speak of injury costs in terms of how many more sales you would have to make to replace the money wasted on injuries. Likewise, if profit is the primary driver, express the costs of injury in terms of the amount by which profit must be increased to cover the cost of injuries. Speaking the language of safety makes safety real to other executives; it explains safety in terms that the other leader can understand but that he or she also values. Years ago I was working with a manufacturer of heavy equipment. The attitude there was "Safety first in the front offices, production first in the shop area". I was talking to a general manager and a supervisor when I casually asked how much money it cost to shut down production. They eagerly told me that if they shut down just their work cell it cost the company about $20,000 a minute! But if the problem was severe enough to shut down the entire plant, the cost jumped to $120,000 a minute in lost production. I knew cost and production were drivers at this particular plant, so I asked them how long the average injury shut things down and they answered (not making the connection) that an average injury usually shut the entire plant down for at least 10 minutes. "Hmmm...," I said, "so the average injury costs the plant $1,200,000 before it is even treated?" They were gobsmacked. They had never before drawn the correlation between injuries and lost production. While previously concerned about the human costs, in an instant they went from being largely indifferent to the hard costs of safety to safety evangelists. In that instant, safety made sense to them and became a value. In another instance a safety supervisor would routinely report out the extra number of products the plant had to build to recoup the lost costs of production caused by injuries and the cost of treating those injuries. Nothing gets the attention of a plant manager, or depot manager, or construction project manager, more than talking about the money that the problem is costing them.

5) Develop big-picture solutions. Becoming an effective safety leader is as much about letting go as it is about acquiring new skills. One of the most difficult transitions in my life was when I moved from being a "single-contributor" to a manager. I liked doing many of the things that my staff were now doing and did a lot of that work alongside them. One day, my boss, the CFO, told me that I would have to stop doing staff work and start working like a manager. It was sort of like being the first chair violinist in an orchestra and getting promoted to conductor – I couldn't do both at once without doing a poor job as the other. The job of the safety leader isn't to buy safety gloves or to figure out the best price for Band-Aids. The job of the safety leader is to develop big-picture safety initiatives that support the company's business model and enable safety to be hard-wired into everything the company does.

156

FROM AUSTRALIA...
Success Is All About How You Show Up

When it comes to leading – whether it be a change in safety or leading in your daily life – a lot of success comes down to how you show up. This sounds pretty basic, and it's almost a quote from Woody Allen who said, "Eighty percent of success is showing up." Sometimes wisdom comes from the strangest places. What Woody Allen missed is that showing up, in and of itself, isn't enough. Most of what's wrong with the world can be traced to people who just showed up long enough for the proverbial attendance to be taken.

When it comes to leading – whether it be a change in safety or leading in your daily life – a lot of success comes down to how you show up. This sounds pretty basic, and it's almost a quote from Woody Allen who said, "Eighty percent of success is showing up." Sometimes wisdom comes from the strangest places. What Woody Allen missed is that showing up, in and of itself, isn't enough. Most of what's wrong with the world can be traced to people who just showed up long enough for the proverbial attendance to be taken.

In the world of Safety, we have a lot of organizations who merely show up. Whether it be safety training or injury record keeping they are primarily interested in getting the magic checkmark of compliance. C work is passing and an A just isn't worth the time or money it takes to get there. That's unfortunate; making a concerted effort to improve how we show up can have a profound impact on the value on which the organization places on safety.

I know there are many of you out there who don't share my view of safety. I see safety as a neglected discipline that has become, to a large extent a bleak wasteland where innovation goes to die, a haven for snake-oil salesmen and quacks, and above all a place inhospitable to change. Most of you who disagree have been professional enough to argue against my position, not my personality, but others....well just keep the hate mail coming. Of course, there are exceptions (I put this in for the buffoons who read my work solely to get themselves into a frothy twist), and I am always delighted to hear about the successes those rarefied few who (despite the odds) champion new ideas and innovative approaches to safety.

Why are these people successful when so many others fail? How can a handful of people advance the profession while so many sit around congratulating each other for doing next to nothing? The successful people care about HOW they show up.

The Shadow of The Leader

The concept of how one shows up isn't new, every bit of business advice from Dress for Success to The Goal addresses the idea that how we are perceived by our peers, our subordinates, and the bosses, is one of the single greatest predictors of success. But how the safety professional shows up may be the lynchpin to the success of the Safety function. Like it or not safety professionals are leaders, and there are people in the organization who love catch us failing to wear our personal protective equipment or to otherwise make us out to be hypocrites and liars. This is where we can make a real difference simply by choosing to show up a bit differently than our natural inclination. We need to rise above the petty crap and set an example. This occurred to me in a discussion forum where one dim bulb just kept making personal attacks and dismissing any point I made as either defensive or obvious. I realized that this pathetic wretch desperately wanted to participate in the discussion but was having difficulty "showing up". He posted comment after comment like a preadolescent that couldn't bear letting someone else have the last word. I admit I provoked him, it's tough not to sling the verbal arrow after several days of email that calls you everything but a child of God. I don't think people want to show up the way that this particular person did, and unfortunately we all squander opportunities to make positive contributions no matter how desperately we may want to.

What Does it Mean to Control How You Show Up?

Showing up is about coming to the situation ready to think and act. How we show up dictates how people will respond to us. I provoke. Most of you are reading this expecting to be provoked. Provocation is my job. When you pick up a trade magazine you are typically reading a piece that was written by a vendor who is an active advertiser (he is trying to sell you a product). How impartial do you imagine the manufacturer of gloves will be in his blistering exposé on the future of Kevlar in glove design? And when you go to a safety conference you will see a carefully tailored message delivered by a professional whose speech has been edited and rewritten by her boss, reading from PowerPoint slides prepared by the marketing department. Such is the state of the safety media. I sell the seeds of discontent. Without loudmouths and blowhards and know-it-alls like me, you are left with infinitely polite pundits who tell you are doing a swell job of it. So that's how I show up.

Some of us don't really show up. Sure we come to work, we show up to collect a paycheck. We go to safety meetings and shrug. We put up safety posters and lead the safety BINGO and we go through the motions because we're either too tired, too lazy, or too frustrated to produce more than carbon dioxide and occasionally methane. And there are a lot of us just skating by content with keeping our injury rate a hair above industry average because Operation doesn't expect or value anything more. We tell ourselves we are doing our best. Well, guess what? We can get a baboon in here to try hard. Sometimes your best isn't good enough, but it's a moot point because typically the people who use "I'm doing my best" as an excuse are operating at a performance level so low that it's tough to say they are trying at all. It's time we each take a hard look and ask if we are really showing up for safety.

Truly showing up is about doing what you think needs doing and doing it because it's your job. Some of us show up by blowing the whistle on a crooked employer because all other attempts to turn the situation around has failed even though doing so means we lose our jobs. Some of us show up with ways to raise awareness about a frequently misunderstood element of safety. Some of us show up by learning the business and looking for ways to partner with Operations to make the workplace both safer AND more efficient. I can't tell you how to show up, but I can tell you that if you are truly honest you will know how you're showing up and whether or not you can be proud of how you are showing up.

It sounds trite, but as I enter my office each morning I challenge myself by asking how I am going to show up. As I prep for meetings, I ask myself which personality is going to show up. Will it be the guy who can't pay attention and is fiddling with the email on his phone or will it be the guy who is fully present and listening to the matters at hand? Will it be the guy who is open and honest or the guy who hides behind honesty as a way bullying other schools of thought into submission? Will it be the guy who advocates for needed change or the guy who sows anarchy just to watch the flames? Will it be the guy who assumes goodness of intentions in others or the one who sees attacks and insults behind every word? I am certainly capable of being all these guys, but I get to decide which one shows up. I am often disappointed by the results but never so much so that I stop trying. I am responsible for my success, and you are responsible for yours. Do you even know that there's a choice?

Never Argue With An Idiot

A few months back I was arguing with some of my many detractors over something I had written in one of the peer-reviewed publications for which I write. My editor gave me a bit of advice, "Never argue with idiots, and these guys are idiots." They weren't, and if I might smugly offer, I don't think many people who read my stuff are idiots; it's too advanced for the truly stupid. But I do deal with a fair amount of fanatics, and fanatics are far more dangerous and destructive to our profession. Fanatics only know one way to show up – angry. Fanatics can't show up without shouting down anyone else in the room; they will tolerate no dissent. Change is evil, any challenge to their doctrine is evil, and attacks are the only response with which they are comfortable.

There are plenty of people who resent being reminded that they could do a much better job controlling who shows up at their jobs, and that's fine. They aren't going to stop being slugs simply because they read something I wrote, and I am not going to stop criticizing someone who collects a paycheck in safety and does nothing but takes up space. But for the vast majority of the safety professionals out there who still care about the state of profession how are you going to show up?

FROM THE MIDDLE EAST AND AFRICA...

Mining Safety

As OHS professionals advance through their careers, they need to become less of an Mining disasters are big news. There is something about men and women buried alive that captures the imagination and horrifies people - and well it should.

Experts worldwide estimate that there are approximately 20,000 mining deaths globally. While that number is difficult to substantiate there is no denying that mining, as a profession, produces more than its fair share of deaths. In fact, the International Labour Organization (ILO) reports that "while mining employs around 1% of the global labour force, it generates 8% of fatal accidents." There's cause for hope as in many countries mining fatalities are on the decrease, but unfortunately in some of the largest countries, most notably China and Russia, mine fatalities are still a major problem.

Unsafe practices

Olivia Lang, a reporter for BBC News, detailed the shocking reality of unsafe practices in mines and the indifference to human life shown by companies in her 14 October 2010 article: The Dangers of Mining around the World . 1 Lang reported that "China has the world's largest mining industry, producing up to three billion tonnes of coal each year.

But while the country accounts for 40% of global coal output, it is responsible for 80% of mining deaths around the world each year." This statistic is made even more chilling by the comments of Alan Baxter, a Fellow of the Institute of Materials, Minerals and Mining, who Olivia interviewed for the article and referenced his comment that in places like China and Russia, the reason for the fatalities is simple: money. In this same article, Alan is reported to have said: "The mentality [in China] is that life is cheaper than it is here and no-one is going to kick up a fuss if they lose a few lives."

Skills shortage

In addition to the intrinsically dangerous work associated with many elements of mining, and the indifference to human life shown by some companies and countries, in many parts of the world there is a shortage of experienced miners. According to the US Mining Safety and Health Administration (MSHA), this shortage of experience miners means that mining companies are forced to hire inexperienced miners. These companies need to design and develop comprehensive training to close the knowledge gap that exists between inexperienced workers and their veteran co-workers.

The training must be comprehensive; a word bandied about so often that it loses its meaning. By 'comprehensive' I mean the training must include:

- A complete orientation of the hazards typically encountered in mining
- All the appropriate PPE associated with working in or around a mine
- Job-specific training on the tasks they will perform
- Specific information on the hazards associated with jobs performed by others working in their proximity
- Identification of hazardous anomalies on the site

Chilling statistics for 2011 provided by the MSHA demonstrate the importance of the role that worker experience plays in mining fatalities:

In 2005 MSHA reported the circumstances of an inexperienced miner's serious injury caused by a lack of thorough and complete training: "A new inexperienced miner was nearly killed due to being hit by a shuttle car. The miner had received training for the roof bolter he was operating but it became evident from the type of accident that a more effective overall training programme should be conducted to include all aspects of the working section."

Protecting miners

The first, and perhaps best, protection a miner can have is a miner in distress device. These devices allow miners to call for help if they become injured and are especially useful in situations where the miner has become incapacitated. Without a means of summoning help the miner might lay undiscovered for hours. Unfortunately, there are severe limitations on most of these devices; chief among these is that for this type of device to work effectively the miner must be signed into a wireless network or have other data plan coverage. Some would argue that miners would be better served with radios, although advocates of miner-in-distress devices counter that radios are often dropped or broken in the incident that has put the miner in distress. Although a bit more costly, the most practical solution is to provide both devices so that there is a redundant system for ensuring first responders can quickly come to the aid of miners in distress.

Much of the PPE needed in mining is the same as that of construction. Unfortunately, according to a survey noted by the MSHA: "A survey of road construction safety leaders estimated that eye protection was being used only half the time it was needed. The same survey said the number one barrier to wearing safety glasses/ goggles was "employers don't require/enforce usage."

From 2000 through 2011, about 3,200 eye injuries occurred in the mining industry. 6 Miners injure their eyes in much the same way that other workers do:

- Airborne particles or debris

- Foreign objects in the eye caused by chemical splashes, dust etc
- By striking their eye against an object or getting poked in the eye with an object

According to MSHA: "studies have shown that 90 percent of all workplace eye injuries can be prevented when miners wear the proper eye protection. Most injuries occur because the miner was not wearing eye protection at the time of the accident. In other instances, miners were wearing eye protection but the eyewear did not adequately protect against the specific hazard involved."

Clearly, wearing the appropriate eye protection is an important defence against eye injuries, but beyond PPE, MSHA warns minors to take additional precautions:

1. **Wear the appropriate eyewear.** When it comes to eye protection all safety glasses are not created equal. When selecting eye protection consider the working environment. If, for example, you are working in an area with high concentrations of dust you should select glasses that are equipped with dust barriers. Similarly, if you are working around welding ensure that you have the proper UV protection for the task that you will be performing

2. **Ensure your glasses fit properly and are comfortable to wear for prolonged periods of time.** PPE is only effective if it fits properly and is worn correctly. Also, it's important that you wear your safety glasses the entire time you are in the work area and that you do not remove them until you are away from the job site. Many foreign particles enter the eyes when workers remove glasses during breaks and place them on a contaminated surface (like a dusty work bench or dirty tool box) the foreign particles get on the glasses and ultimately end up in the worker's eye. Storing your safety glasses in a place where they remain clean and undamaged is a key to avoiding eye injuries.

Not much can be said about PPE in terms of preventing injury or death in the initial disaster – which can range from cave-ins to explosions of trapped pockets of natural gas. If worker is in the direct line of fire when disaster strikes the likelihood of survival is slight, but that's not to say that PPE in mines isn't important, or even essential in surviving.

Perhaps the most difficult aspect of saving imperilled lives in a mining disaster is getting to the miners who weren't necessarily injured by the initial event, but who are now trapped in the mine because the catastrophic event has blocked their egress route. Miners needlessly die because they lack the PPE that would otherwise keep them alive until they could be rescued.

Surviving disasters

Surviving a catastrophic mining accident begins by being prepared before the incident occurs. A good Emergency Action Plan (EAP) is essential and should include:

1. Clear identification of the 'person-in-charge' of both the Emergency Action Plan (EAP), and the chain-of-command. When everyone is responsible for something, then no one is really responsible. A good EAP will identify the ultimate owner of the plan and a chain-of-command so that everyone knows who will be doing what, and who assumes an absent team member's duties.
2. Evacuation procedures and identification of all exit routes. In general, a single evacuation route is neither advisable nor effective, but in many cases geography may limit your ability to have an alternate evacuation route. The evacuation route should identify rally points where workers gather after the site has been evacuated so all workers can be accounted for.
3. First-aid and rescue duty assignments. All miners should be provided an orientation that identifies the first responders and how to contact them. Ideally this information should be posted in multiple locations so that the information is readily accessible.
4. Methods of reporting emergencies by any employee. A system must be developed so that any and all employees have the right and ability

to sound the alarm that an emergency has occurred. This system need not be sophisticated or expensive, but it should be tested to ensure that it is effective.

5. Procedures for employees who remain behind. In some cases, some workers will be required to remain behind to shut off equipment, ensure toxic or explosive chemicals are secured, or wait with an injured worker until first responders arrive. In these cases, strict protocols designed to subject these workers to the lowest possible risk are essential.

6. Procedures for accounting of all employees after evacuation, or upon a shelter-in-place emergency. Once at the rally point, the person in charge of implementing the EAP must have a means of quickly ascertaining who is present and who is absent. Often first responders needlessly risk their lives, and even lose them, looking for someone who had already vacated the premises.

7. Procedures for critical operation shutdown. In many cases, the mine simply cannot be hastily abandoned and critical operations must be shut down before the mine can be evacuated. The emergency plan must clearly identify the "who?" "what?" "why?" "where?" and "how long?" of the procedure for shutting down critical operations.

Having an EAP in itself does nothing to protect workers; you must communicate it. One of the best ways of communicating an EAP is through a rigorous process of drills. Frequent drills change behaviours that require a lot of thinking and decision making into unconscious habits that require little to no thinking or decision making. When an emergency strikes time is of the essence and the fewer decisions that need to be made the more likely workers are going to escape danger unscathed.

Another important aspect of mining safety is your understanding the triggers of the most serious incidents and doing your utmost to recognise and avoid triggering catastrophes and reminding co-workers to do the same. Hard hats can protect you from the occasional falling object, but will offer little protection if tons of stone cave in on you.

Daily safety

Much of mining safety relies on you and the decisions you make throughout your work day. To improve your safety and the safety of others remember to:

1. **Use Stop Work Authority**. Never forget that there is always some level of risk of injury in every workplace and that risk is much higher in mining than in other work environments. Never undertake a job or perform a task that you believe could be unsafe. Stopping work doesn't mean that you necessarily halt all work at the mine – it could be as simple as double checking that you are correctly wearing all your PPE or that you are using the correct tool for the jobs.

2. **Plan, plan, plan.** There is an expression among carpenters: measure twice, cut once. It means that by thoroughly and completely planning a job you can avoid costly – and in the case of safety, deadly – mistakes later. A plan is only a piece of paper, however, unless you put it into action and communicate how the plan will be executed to all those around you. If something changes or if there is something present that you failed to anticipate in your plan, then revise it. Plans should be living documents that are never complete until the last miner goes home safely.

   When you are planning remember to build-in safety to your plan. This probably will mean that you will have to take extra time to ensure that safety checks are made. Remember, planning to do the job safely may be time consuming, but far less so than a serious injury or a fatality on the site.

3. **PPE isn't optional.** Wearing your PPE isn't optional it's mandatory, not just for you but for everyone around you. Sometimes our poor choices put other people's safety at risk, not just our own. If you see someone who isn't wearing the appropriate PPE remind him or her and if he or she doesn't like it then so be it. Better to have them

irritated by you than for them to die because you stood by and said nothing.

4. **Don't do a job unless you are satisfied that you are qualified to do it safely.** This can be tricky. Nobody wants to admit that they are a little shaky on the details of a task that is core to their job responsibilities but being capable of doing the job correctly is the single greatest safety tool at your disposal. Recognise that just because you sat at a computer screen or a boring safety training doesn't necessarily mean that you can do your job. If you are unsure of a task or procedure ask your supervisor and keep asking until you are certain you can do the job safely.

5. **Follow ALL the safety rules.** Sometimes the rules don't make any sense. Sometimes the rules seem silly and over protective. Sometimes the rules are maddening, but however you feel about the rules follow them: everyone, every job, every time.

About the Author

A self-described provocateur and iconoclast, Phil La Duke has poked and prodded the word of safety asking those awkward questions about some of the Safety professions most sacred truisms and indelicately pointing out flaws in long established and accepted safety practices. Phil La Duke is an itinerant pot stirrer, internationally renowned executive consultant, safety expert, speaker, blogger, trainer, and business author. He frequently guest lectures at universities including presentations at Tulane, Loyola, the University of Michigan, and Johns Hopkins and is on the Wayne State Biomedical Safety Board. With over 250 published works in print, La Duke, has contributed content to numerous notable magazines and is published on all inhabited continents. Mr. La Duke's take-no-prisoners style garnered him positions on *Industrial Safety and Hygiene News* (ISHN) magazine's Power 101 (a list of the world's most influential people working in worker safety) and its list of Up and Comers in Safety Thought Leadership.

All reprints of blog posts have been approved for reprinting for this book.

*Original blog posts sources

Safety: The View From The Outside In
(Originally posted on May 20, 2018, in Phil La Duke's blog, it can be found
here:https://philladuke.wordpress.com/2018/05/20/safety-the-view-from-the-outside-in/

An Open Letter to Safety Professionals from the 4,690 Workers Who Died on the Job in the United States in 2010
(Originally posted on May 5, 2012, in Phil La Duke's blog, it can be found here:
https://philladuke.wordpress.com/2012/05/05/an-open-letter-to-safety-professionals-from-the-4690-workers-who-died-on-the-job-in-the-united-states-in-2010/

What's Wrong With Safety Training . . . And How To Fix It
(The initial date of publication is lost in the blogosphere but in December 13 2011. it was re-run in F&M and can be found here
http://www.fabricatingandmetalworking.com/2011/12/whats-wrong-with-safety-training-and-how-to-fix-it/ **Reprinted with permission.**

Four Reasons, Eight Lessons
(Originally published in Facility Safety Management **April 2011. Used with permission.**

Spitting on Forest Fires
(Originally posted on May 9, 2018, in Phil La Duke's blog, it can be found here:
https://philladuke.wordpress.com/2018/05/09/spitting-on-forest-fires/

Your Mother Doesn't Work Here: Why Housekeeping Matters
(Originally published by *Fabricating & Metalworking* **magazine** on **September 20, 2013)**
The original can be found here: http://www.fabricatingandmetalworking.com/2013/09/your-mother-doesnt-work-here-why-housekeeping-matters/

The Rise of the Safety Jihadist
(Originally published on www.philladuke.wordpress.com **7:27 am on February 19, 2018)**
The original can be found here https://wordpress.com/post/philladuke.wordpress.com/6089

The 14 Points of Workplace Safety
Deming On Safety

(Originally published September 13, 2012, in Fabricating & Metalworking it can be found here: https://workersafetynet.wordpress.com/2011/07/17/deming-on-safety-part-1-constancy-of-purpose-for-safety/) Reprinted with permission.

Deming On Safety Point 1: Constancy of Purpose For Safety
(Originally published July 17, 2011, on The Safety Net blog it can be found here: https://workersafetynet.wordpress.com/2011/07/17/deming-on-safety-part-1-constancy-of-purpose-for-safety/)

More Deming On Safety: Adopt the New Philosophy
(Orginally published on www.philladuke.wordpress.com on September 18, 2011, it can be found here https://wordpress.com/post/philladuke.wordpress.com/457

Point 4: Instill Universal Ownership and Accountability for Safety
(Originally published May 12, 2012, on The Safety Net blog it can be found here: https://workersafetynet.wordpress.com/?s=point+2)

Deming On Safety Point 5: Improve The System
(Originally published January 28, 2012, on The Safety Net blog it can be found here: https://workersafetynet.wordpress.com/2012/01/28/deming-on-safety-pt-5/

Deming On Safety Pt. 6: Point 6 Institute Training On the Job
Originally published February 4, 2012, on my blog Worker Safety Net it can be found here https://workersafetynet.wordpress.com/2012/02/04/deming-on-safety-pt-6-point-5-institute-training-on-the-job/

Deming On Safety: Part 8
Originally published on May 5, 2012, on my Worker Safety Net blog it can be found here: https://workersafetynet.wordpress.com/2012/05/05/deming-on-safety-part-8/

Deming On Safety Point 11
(Originally published August 5,, 2012, on The Safety Net blog it can be found here: https://workersafetynet.wordpress.com/2012/08/05/deming-on-safety-the-eleventh-point/

Deming on Safety Point 12 "Remove Barriers To Pride Of Workmanship"
(Originally posted on the Worker Safety Net blog it can be found here: https://workersafetynet.wordpress.com/2012/08/11/deming-on-safety-point-11-remove-barriers-to-pride-of-workmanship/)

Deming on Safety: The 13th Point

(Originally posted on the Worker Safety Net blog on October 7, 2012, it can be found here: https://workersafetynet.wordpress.com/2012/10/07/deming-on-safety-the-13th-point/

Deming on Safety Point 14: The Transformation is Everyone's Job

DECEMBER 1, 2012 https://workersafetynet.wordpress.com/2012/12/01/deming-on-safety-point-14-the-transformation-is-everyones-job/

A Pyramid By Any Other Name

(Originally published on February 14 2014 it can be found here: https://philladuke.wordpress.com/2015/02/14/a-pyramid-by-any-other-name/)

The Rise of the Safety Extremist

(Originally published on February 14 2014 it can be found here: https://philladuke.wordpress.com/2013/06/16/4250/)

The Power of Pyramids: How Using Outmoded Thinking About Hazards Can Be Deadly

(Originally published on August 30 2014 it can be found here: https://philladuke.wordpress.com/2014/08/30/the-power-of-pyramids-how-using-outmoded-thinking-about-hazards-can-be-deadly/)

The Basics of Safety: Behavior-Based Safety vs. Process-Based Safety

(Originally published in *Fabricating & Metalworking Magazine on November 26, 2012,* it can be found here: http://www.fabricatingandmetalworking.com/2012/11/the-basics-of-safetybehavior-based-safety-vs-process-based-safety/2/)

Why Behavior Based Safety Will Live Forever

(Originally published on December 29, 2014 it can be found here: https://wordpress.com/post/philladuke.wordpress.com/4670)

Four Flaws of Behavior-Based Safety

(Originally published on July 3, 2011 it can be found here: https://philladuke.wordpress.com/2011/07/03/four-flaws-of-behavior-based-safety/)

What's Wrong With Drinking The Kool-Aid?

(Originally published on May 6, 2015 it can be found here: https://philladuke.wordpress.com/2015/05/06/whats-wrong-with-drinking-the-kool-aid/)

Everyone Is An Idiot Except Me

(Originally published in October on blog *The Safety Net* The origional can be found here
https://workersafetynet.wordpress.com/2011/11/12/everyone-is-an-idiot-but-me/

Safety Slogans Don't Save Lives

(Originally published April 1, 2015, in Industrial Safety & Hygeine News (ISHN), the origional article can be found here
https://workersafetynet.wordpress.com/2011/11/12/everyone-is-an-idiot-but-me/ reprinted with permission

Asleep on the Job: The lethal connection between falls from height and sleep deprivation

(Originally published 19th Mar 2014 in Health and Safety International can be found here
https://www.hsimagazine.com/article/asleep-on-the-job-1032)

5 Steps To Becoming A More Successful Safety Leader

(Originally published Mar 2017 in OHSProfessional it can be found here
https://www.hsimagazine.com/article/asleep-on-the-job-1032)

Success Is All About How You Show Up

(Originally published March 22, 2012, as an exclusive in the world's foremost safety blog: This post (as well as many other of my posts that can only be found here) can be found here in
https://safetyrisk.net/success-is-all-about-how-you-show-up/

Mining Safety

(Originally published 11/08/2016 in HSME it can be found here
https://www.hsmemagazine.com/article/mining-safety-1251)

Made in the USA
Middletown, DE
29 January 2019